P9-BJH-030

DARK PASSAGES

VANISHING SHIPS OF THE PACIFIC OCEAN

II DARK PASSAGES

DARK PASSAGES

Vanishing Ships of the Pacific Ocean

by
David H. Grover

THE GLENCANNON PRESS

MARITIME BOOKS

El Cerrito
2011

This book is copyright © 2011.

Published by The Glencannon Press
P.O. Box 1428, El Cerrito, CA 94302
Tel. 800-711-8985, Fax. 510-528-3194
www.glencannon.com

First Edition, first printing.

ISBN 978-1-889901-52-7

Library of Congress Cataloging-in-Publication Data

Grover, David H. (David Hubert), 1925-
  Dark passages : vanishing ships of the Pacific Ocean / by David H.
Gro-   ver. -- 1st ed.
      p. cm.
  Includes bibliographical references and index.
  ISBN 978-1-889901-52-7 (alk. paper)
1. Ships--Pacific Ocean--History--20th century. 2. Pacific Ocean--History,
Naval--20th century. 3. Curiosities and wonders--Pacific Ocean--History--
20th century. 4 Disappearances (Parapsychology)--Pacific Ocean--History
--20th century. 5. Seafaring life--Pacific Ocean--History--20th century. I.
Title.
  G557.G76 2011
  910.9164-dc22
                              2011008848

Publisher's notes:
Every effort is made to obtain and reproduce the best quality photographs.
Due to wartime conditions, and the age of the photos available, a number
are of lesser quality. They have nevertheless been used.

All rights reserved. Printed in the United States of America. No part of this
book may be used or reproduced, stored in a retrieval system, or transmitted
in any form or by any means, electronic, mechanical, photocopying, recording
or otherwise in any manner whatsoever without written permission except
in the case of brief quotations embodied in critical articles or reviews.

Dedication

In memory of our son
Jeff, who showed us
what courage is all about,
this book is lovingly dedicated.

Also by the author:

Debaters and Dynamiters: The Story of the Haywood Trial

Diamonfield Jack, A Study in Frontier Justice

Landmarks in Western Oratory (editor)

U.S. Army Ships and Watercraft of World War II

Captives of Shanghai: The Story of the President Harrison (with Gretchen G. Grover)

American Merchant Ships on the Yangtze, 1920-1941

Voices from the Yangtze (editor, via pseudonym Jeffrey St. John)

The San Francisco Shipping Conspiracies of World War One

The Unforgiving Coast: Maritime Disasters of the Pacific Northwest

CONTENTS

FOREWORD

This book grew out of an earlier effort to capture some of the heartbreak and mystery of maritime disasters, specifically those of a number of ships that were lost in the Pacific Northwest early in the 20th century. That book was titled *The Unforgiving Coast: Maritime Disasters of the Pacific Northwest.* Its chapters described a series of tragic incidents consisting of groundings, founderings, a fire at sea, and in one case the disappearance of a ship.

When that book was finished the final incident, the disappearance of the steam schooner *South Coast*, would not go away. Ship disappearances are haunting experiences for relatives of those who have been lost, and for society in general. For those of us who investigate these events it is easy to become caught up in them to the point where we are often compelled to look further in the hope of turning up some overlooked detail that might point toward solving the mystery of the vanishing ship.

Such was the early rationale for this work. Its author, after finishing that earlier book, once attempted a broader genre, a comprehensive but never published shipwreck book in which it was necessary periodically to invoke the name of the *Titanic* and that of USS *Cyclops*. He is now testing the waters with the narrower genre of ship disappearances in the Pacific, mostly in the first half of 20th century. Today, lacking a proper giant with which to compare ship disappearances on this great ocean that covers so much of our planet, the name to drop might well be that of the relatively unknown *Cynthia Olson*, the first American merchant ship to vanish in World War II and perhaps one of only a few such ships whose fate still remains in question. Indeed, that ship and her disappearance in the eastern Pacific is described within these pages.

In several other chapters the mystery to be described is not just that of a simple ship disappearance, if indeed there is such a thing, but rather the existence of an *aura* of mystery surrounding a ship that seems to affect other vessels with which she comes in contact. This contact may lead to both the disappearance and reappearance of other vessels, as well as to a "now-you-see-her-now-you-don't" *persona* for the ship in question.

No particular sequence suggests itself in telling these true tales, so the chapters are presented in chronological order. In each case an effort has been made to understand the nature and feelings of the crewmen caught up in these mysteries, but research sources for many of the vessels unfortunately do not provide enough information to personalize the crew to any degree.

Generally speaking, each chapter was written at a different time, and some months may have elapsed between the writing of some of them. Consequently, there may not be the uniformity in approach or comparability of analysis that a reader might expect. This disparity, however, serves a useful purpose in showing that there is no standard formula by which a series of complex events with human, mechanical, and geographical dimensions can be analyzed, or compared with seemingly similar events.

An author venturing into this genre is soon struck with the reality that original sources, particularly eye-witness accounts, are not available. Conjecture, which has lured many a maritime historian into unwise conclusions, is the only tool available to the writer searching further for insights into vessels for whom the search has long been abandoned, both literally and figuratively.

If, in the pages that follow, well-reasoned conjecture sometimes gives way to what the reader considers to be rash and unwarranted conclusions, the author takes full responsibility. Furthermore, he encourages readers to create alternative scenarios of their own for the fate of the various ships.

Each of the chapters in this book is devoted to a maritime mystery about a ship and her crew, and to the oddities of fate that led to their disappearance or demise. While the circumstances of these events were not totally unknown at the time the author first chose to write about them, his treatment in earlier published accounts, generally in maritime history magazines, has been largely responsible for each mystery coming together as a focused and discrete entity. In other words, the earlier writing has given substance and consequence to the mystery, while noting the lack of attention given to the event by the maritime historical community.

Research for this book has been conducted through the standard sources of maritime literature and institutions, coupled with a growing use of internet sources which can, if not used judiciously, add another layer of uncertainty to the accumulated information. Among the museums and archives utilized are the San Francisco Maritime National Historical Park, the Puget Sound Maritime Historical Society, the Steamship Historical Society of America, the Mariners Museum, the Naval Historical Center, the National Archives in Washington and regionally in San Bruno, California, and Seattle, Washington. Library collections consulted include those of the California Maritime Academy, the University of California at Davis, Sonoma State University, the University of Washington, the U. S. Naval Postgraduate School, and the Napa Public Library.

Several individuals were helpful in the research on West Coast ships, particularly the late James Mossman of the Puget Sound Maritime Historical Society in Seattle who assisted on a number of the author's writing projects, and William Kooiman of the San Francisco Maritime Museum who also provided valuable assistance in the past. Special insights were also provided by fellow author, Charles Dana Gibson, and editorial assistance was supplied by the author's daughter, Rebecca Grover Anderson, who helped untangle more than one computer glitch.

A few corporate sources were also consulted, namely Alexander & Baldwin, owners of the Matson Line whose *Lurline* was an electronic witness to the disappearance of one of the ships in this book, and the Wheelock Company of Hong Kong which owned another of the vanished ships.

Each of the author's earlier books of maritime history has made use of new technologies of writing and publishing as they have appeared. Over the quarter century corresponding to that output, the author has moved from the type-and-paste era into practices quite different from those we learned in our collegiate days, and into new technologies, principally the computer, and new sources of information, to wit the internet. The transition has sometimes been difficult, but somehow we've made it, and are gratified today that style manuals such as that of the Modern Language Association tell us how to cite even such things as websites in our endnotes and bibliographies.

Speaking of websites, the internet sites which were utilized in this book are listed in the notes and bibliography. Several such sites should also be singled out because of their ongoing usefulness to maritime historians. These include the definitive merchant marine site found at www.usmm.org and the extensive shipbuilding site at www.coltoncompany.com, as well as the naval vessel sites at www.hazegray.com and www.navsource.com. The author is convinced that the internet, in spite of its obvious limitations in research, will increasingly become the means whereby researchers discover new avenues of exploration.

With these formalities and credits out of the way, we are ready to examine the world of vanishing ships and other mysteries of the deep. Moving into the initial chapter of the book with its broad-brush treatment of that world, bear in mind that ship disappearances and other bizarre happenings that ships encounter are not just abstract and ill-dated historical events. They are also true mysteries, akin to the great mysteries of life itself, and characterized by the loss of many innocent seafarers who did not deserve to die. May this awareness go with you in exploring the pages that lie ahead.

XVI DARK PASSAGES

1

CHARTING THE
COURSE

A century ago the great chronicler of life at sea, Joseph Conrad, observed in his novel *Typhoon* that "The sea never changes and its works, for all the talk of men, are wrapped in mystery." Indeed, most men who have been drawn to the sea, even for only part of their lives, would agree that there is the potential for mystery in every moment as a ship makes her way across the lonely stretches of the great oceans of the world.

While such mysteries can take many forms, there is perhaps nothing in the broad genre of literature of the sea, either historical or fictional, more intriguing on one hand and more chilling and sobering on the other than the story of a ship which has vanished with all hands, while leaving no readable clues to her fate.

While ships still occasionally "go missing," that event is rare today compared to the first half of the 20th century when it was an all-too-common occurrence. War, of course, has always been a great stimulus to the disappearance of ships. The lack of a war at sea for sixty-five years (other than the Falkland Islands War which was a very specialized situation) has drastically reduced the existence of such mysteries, and no one could properly regret that reduction. Better reporting and better detection of vessels in peacetime have further reduced the number of disappearances.

In 1961, sixteen years after the end of hostilities of World War II, the authoritative *Proceedings* published by the U. S. Naval Institute ran an article by Lt. Cdr. Edward F. Oliver of the U. S. Coast Guard in which appeared brief accounts of nineteen ships which, as of that date, were still "Overdue, Presumed Lost" from the war.[1]

Today, seventeen of those ships can be removed from that list, largely because the records of German U-boats and Japanese submarines which are now widely available, although absolute proof of the status of one of these missing ships and the fate of her crew is still lacking.

That ship will be examined in the following pages, along with other missing ships from both World Wars, the Sino-Japanese War, and that happy interlude we knew as peacetime. The ships to be reviewed were chosen for their diversity, and for the interesting circumstances surrounding their disappearances and the strange milieus into which they sailed.

It is difficult to maintain a balanced perspective in analyzing the disappearance of ships. In one sense, when a ship vanishes it is a routine daily event, as ships simply sail beyond the horizon and are lost to viewers ashore or afloat. Similarly, a ship being observed on a radar screen can "disappear," not by sinking but by the simple expedient of sailing beyond the range of the radar and its screen. Thus, the word "disappear" has a mundane workaday connotation which may interfere with a reader's ability to comprehend the larger and more sinister meaning of the term.

At the other end of the spectrum of meaning there are emotional images conjured up by the term that rise well above those created by ships merely being out of sight. These images ignore the harsher realities of physical disappearance in an effort to capture the excitement of such an event. For some people there is a type of perverse romanticism in imagining ships that have vanished from the earth as having achieved some sort of glory or nirvana. This misguided romanticism may have originated with the disappearance of planes and aviators at sea as in the case of such adventurers as the team of Amelia Earhart and Fred Noonan and others who have deliberately pursued dangerous goals. Their disappearance has generated an aura of noble heroism.

Afloat, that spirit has perhaps best been personified in the romantic figure of Richard Halliburton, the young American adventurer and writer who in 1939 was lost at sea while trying to sail a Chinese junk across the Pacific. Others, such as Joshua Slocum, who have engaged in solo sailing or rowing trips across oceans or even around the world are of this same breed.

That notion of the heroic spawns further reactions ranging from ethereal images of intrepid men sailing off into a sunset that symbolizes the unknown, or of early marine explorers achieving the status of legends by vanishing while in search of "new worlds to conquer," which happens to be the title of one of Halliburton's books.

The reality, all too easily overlooked, is that what we must contemplate in the disappearance of a ship is a human tragedy of sobering proportions. When this tragedy occurs, dozens of helpless men are left alone in the vastness of an ocean, not because of their pursuit of some romantic goal but because their job or their duty carried them into harm's way. There, too often, they die a horrible death, with no one aware of their peril or their presence.

A ship at sea is more than simply a complicated piece of machinery used in transporting a cargo. It is a community of men who often were total strangers at the beginning of a voyage. For these men the ship is a home, just as fully as a cottage ashore would be. It is also their workplace, the source of their livelihood. It even becomes their nationality, permanently or transiently, as a small outpost of the nation whose flag flies aboard her and whose protection they expect to enjoy. With the loss of a ship comes the loss of all these relationships.

Quite possibly, the surest way to appreciate the realistic rather than the mystic aspects of a disappearing ship would be to put oneself in the position of having had a loved one aboard the doomed vessel. In the adventures of the ships that appear in this book there will be moments that evoke a wide variety of emotions. There will also be inexplicable events, to which it is difficult to know how to react. In trying to minimize those confusing moments, as well as in laying out what it is this book proposes to do, it may be useful to define several key terms before exploring further the nature of a ship's disappearance. To avoid descending into a trivial level of categories and distinctions, examples from the real world of vanishing ships will be utilized to illustrate points whenever possible.

Perhaps it would be wise at the outset to speak of ships that *vanish* as a more comprehensive verb than *disappear*. Unfortunately, however, grammarians have failed to provide us with a convenient noun form of that verb as evocative and comfortable as *disappearance* for the act of *disappearing*. Neither writer nor reader is likely to be prepared to cope with *vanishment* for the act of *vanishing*. The same unwieldiness occurs in trying to convert *gone missing* into a noun form. Thus, by default, *disappear* becomes the verb of choice.

The focus of the book will be largely on American ships, a choice dictated both by reader interest and by the desire to keep research within manageable geographical limits. Virtually all the ships included in this book were American-flag ships for much, if not all, of their service (and a number served in the United States Navy or Army). Several, were reflagged in friendly foreign countries shortly before their disappearance, and all departed from North American ports.

The time frame chosen for this book, the half-century between 1900 and 1950, corresponds to the beginnings of widespread use of radio aboard ship, and extends through the impact of two world wars, to arrive at a leavening period of peacetime in which the technological advances of the second of those world wars came into widespread use among new generations of ships. Thus, the full range of defenses against disappearing can be explored in a variety of circumstances.

With all the possible routes that a book such as this might travel, it is wise to focus on one that is realistic and achievable. Determining the cause of each ship's disappearance, or, more analytically, solving each mystery, is beyond that set of intentions, and will not be one of the intended outcomes. However, adding to the available information surrounding the circumstances of each ship's final moments will, with any luck, be an attainable result, at least for some of the ships.

The common terminology for the disappearance of a ship includes the phrase "without a trace." However, we can readily establish that no ship vanishes utterly without a trace, because her departure from port, administratively and physically, indicates where she is going. Her clearance, which is her authorization to leave port, or her orders if a naval vessel, lists a destination, and her physical departure from port includes the establishment of an initial heading or course, readily observed by others, that suggests in broad terms which direction she intends to go. Small and tentative as these clues may be, they are a beginning in understanding where a ship might have been lost, even though these initial clues in themselves may be the final and only such indications of her location.

Sometimes, however, initial general directions can be misleading in determining where a missing ship went. In 1921 the Navy's seagoing tug *Conestoga* went missing while en route from San Francisco to Hawaii and Samoa. The only clue to her disappearance was one of her lifeboats which was found in the vicinity of Clarion Island off the Mexican Coast, south-southeast of her starting point. That location was far from the southwesterly and southerly routes normally steered to reach Hawaii and Samoa. Her disappearance remains a total mystery.[2]

Furthermore, there are times when the disappearance of a ship is not accepted as a reality by the researchers who examine the facts surrounding such an event. Several cases cited in this book have resulted in considerable disagreement as to the fate of the ship. In such cases one group of researchers may typically argue that a ship was torpedoed and lost; sometimes even a time and place are provided. However, no corroboration exists for these sinking in the fairly complete records of submarines and raiders, and researchers cannot point to any other evidence that the ship actually sank. Consequently, the researchers in the other, more prudent, camp respond by citing the only verifiable fact — that the ship has disappeared — and make no pretense of knowing any more.

In still other cases the basic facts may be in dispute. In one instance not reviewed in this book, the sailing date of a convoy varies by three or four weeks in the several accounts of a tanker's alleged sinking, while the Navy was not even sure that the ship had ever been in the convoy. Furthermore, the submarine which is sometimes given credit for sinking the vessel was known to have sunk only two ships during the entire war, neither of which was the ship in question.

Vanishing appears to be a kind of total action in that there are no partial or semi-disappearances of ships. However, it might be argued that there is a temporal factor in disappearance, in that a ship might disappear and reappear. This could happen if she were, say, caught in an icepack in the Arctic. This was the fate of the Hudson Bay Company's steamer *Baychimo* beginning in late 1931, drifting around, out of sight of any observer, until eventually she reappeared somewhere else. This ship, after a half dozen sightings, was last seen thirty-eight years after her drift began. Thus, she had become a lost — and found — ship repeatedly, and she may still be out there to be found again.[3]

Similarly, a former German U-boat, later belonging to the Japanese Navy, broke away from her tug while being towed, and drifted around the Pacific for two years before being sighted in 1927 by two American freighters a thousand miles apart, one of which then scuttled her as a hazard to navigation.[4] Presumably, her status had been that of a vanished vessel, but her scuttling took her off that list and put her on the list of sunken vessels.

Such distinctions can be important. For purposes of insurance settlements and other judicial matters affecting both a ship and her crew, the disappearance of a vessel can create

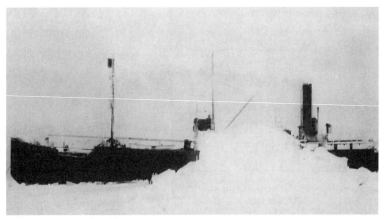

The Baychimo, *taken while she was trapped in ice in 1931. Operated by the Hudson Bay Company, she would disappear and reappear for the next thirty-one years.* www.wikipedia.com.

legal distinctions similar to those created in the disappearance of a person. Proof is generally lacking in such matters; instead the act of disappearance must be deduced through reasonable presumption or circumstantial evidence. However, those disappearances that leave distinct clues to their cause, such as a foundering, are not total disappearances in the true sense. For example, if ships which respond to a distress signal go to the last known position of a ship in peril and then find only a large oil slick, as the SS *Liberator* did in the Pacific in 1927 in search of the SS *Elkton*,[5] the inference can be drawn with some degree of certainty that the ship has gone down. Likewise, if considerable identifiable debris is in the water or washes ashore on a nearby beach, the presumption of a sinking may be even stronger. It is, however, still a presumption.

The point here is that a ship that truly disappears is one whose presumed loss, in the absence of consistent evidence of cause, might have taken one of several yet-to-be-determined forms. There was even a time when a disappearance did not always lead to a presumed demise; in earlier eras a ship could vanish and simply drift around in the form of a ghost ship such as the *Flying Dutchman*, or in a more modern sense drift unseen for an extended time as did the *Baychimo* and the former German U-boat cited above. One ship in this book, the *Maverick,* vanished by all accounts, and yet later reappeared as a ghost ship, making herself known to no less than three other ships.[6] However, today, with surveillance satellites covering the surface of the earth it is unlikely the hull of a drifting ship or a ship seeking to avoid detection would remain undetected for very long.

A temporal dimension also exists in the disappearance of a ship in determining what is a realistic expectation of how long the ship might be regarded as "unreported" rather than declared lost. Such determinations are matters of how much fuel, food, and water remains aboard the vessel, or what chance she has of reaching a benevolent shore where the crewmen can survive, even though they might not be able to communicate immediately.

The totality of a vessel's disappearance should logically extend to all the crewmen and anyone else aboard. Otherwise, the survival of a single such person can, and sometimes does, provide the only information authorities receive regarding the fate of a vessel. The question of what happened to the SS *Stanvac Calcutta*, a tanker that disappeared in World War II, was resolved when a seaman in the ship's crew wrote from a German prison camp to the parent oil company, asking if he could be sent some shoes and cigarettes. Until that letter arrived, the world had no inkling as to the fate of the ship — which had in fact been sunk at the hands of a surface raider which then took prisoners, most of whom ended up incommunicado in Japanese prison camps. The seaman, Sahidi Hassan, was wounded, and, after the surface raider sank, was taken aboard a German blockade runner which

The Stanvac Calcutta *was thought to have vanished until one of her crew, a POW, wrote home for shoes and cigarettes.* aukevisser.nl

brought him to France where he was sent for medical treatment to a prisoner-of-war camp in Germany. His letter ultimately led American authorities to discover the true fate of the ship and her remaining crewmen in Japan who were liberated at the end of the war.[7]

Some of the greatest sagas of the seas have come from a few men who survived disasters through incredible courage and stamina, and were able to tell their inspirational stories. Similarly, a number of the great small-boat voyages of maritime history were made to reveal the existence of a group of survivors on some inhospitable shore, and to insure their ultimate rescue.

Thus, the totality of ship and crew is separable under certain circumstances. When the fate of one is known without the other, there still remains a disappearance and a mystery. The classic example of the ship surviving without her crew is that of the *Mary Celeste* in 1872, and another conspicuous example appears later in the pages of this book. There are many cases of the opposite occuring, that is, the crew has survived without knowing the ultimate fate of their ship.

There are even times when neither ship nor crew survive, but the fate of one is known through valid reports. This circumstance was exemplified in the case of the *Pennsylvania* of the States Steamship Co. which in 1953, shortly after leaving the Pacific Northwest, radioed that a serious crack had developed in the hull, and that the crew was taking to the lifeboats.[8] Neither the vessel nor the crew were ever found, but the fate of the ship seems clearly established.

A variation on this possibility which becomes humiliating for those involved occurs when the crew abandon a vessel which they believe sinking, only to learn later that the vessel has survived as a derelict, and has been taken over by someone else. Joseph Conrad's novel *Lord Jim* is woven against this kind of backdrop, as a young ship's officer must redeem himself for abandoning his post.[9]

Oversights on the part of planners or of a ship's crew can increase the risk that a ship in peril will go unreported. Certainly, the lack of a radio has been a contributory cause in many such cases, particularly before 1920 when shipboard wireless first became a common feature on ocean-going vessels. However, inasmuch as radio capability in its early days mandated the additional cost of a licensed operator, some ships after that date continued without wireless as an economy measure; this was true aboard the frugal *South Coast*, a steam schooner which went missing off the Oregon coast in 1929.[10]

The presence of a radio aboard ship, of course, is no guarantee of communication with shore stations or other ships. Radios must be strong enough to emit a good signal, and kept in good repair. The radio operators of that earlier era were generally not technicians, but rather, artisans who could read and often recognize the "hand' of fellow operators. Furthermore, in disasters the operator had to reach the transmitter and stay with it long enough to get an acknowledgment that his outgoing message was received, thus insuring that the signal actually left the vessel.

An antenna for low-frequency use is relatively easy to rig between two masts of a steamship, but it can be a fragile and vulnerable part of wireless transmission and reception of messages, subject to failure if explosions or violent winds affect the rigging. Likewise, the radio "shack" on many vessels is readily identifiable by the leads that go to it from the antenna, making it possible for gunners on hostile ships or submarines to target it first for silencing.

Radio messages which report on events affecting the safety of a ship are no better than the reporting mechanisms that relay these messages to responsible authorities. The last message from the SS *Cynthia Olson*, one of the vessels described in this book, was picked up and relayed by the Matson liner *Lurline*, but that ship's operator had a difficult time raising a responsible Navy operator in the San Francisco bay area, because it was a Sunday — the Sunday of the Pearl Harbor attack. (In a commentary on the lack of American alertness at that time, one of the books about that seminal event was titled *At Dawn We Slept*.) Finally, the ship's operator reached a commercial short-wave operator to whom the news was passed.[11]

Distress messages have always received the highest priority, ranging from professional operators at the shore facilities of great commercial stations of that era operated by such companies as A. T. & T., Mackay, Globe, *et al*, to the rankest of amateurs. However, the links ashore for conveying merchant ship messages, particularly in peacetime, have not always existed as fully as might be desired. Elaborate networks which report merchant ship casualties, the most famous of which is that of Lloyds of London, have existed for several centuries, but they are designed to provide information well after the fact, and usually are not fast enough to alert the maritime world in time to launch search planes or vessels, or to otherwise be on the lookout for vessels that are unreported but perhaps still afloat.

Prompt initial reporting by the responsible steamship company or maritime agency also helps in preventing or solving cases of apparent disappearance. In 1926 when the SS *Suduffco* vanished on an inter-coastal voyage from New York her owners waited a month before reporting her non-arrival at the Panama Canal.[12] Earlier reporting might have alerted ships to be on the lookout for her or indications of her demise. However, reluctance to report promptly on such non-arrivals is evident in a number of similar instances; it seems as if the concerned party is trying to avoid "crying wolf" by being overly cautious in not seeking help in situations where it might be needed.

Related to the reporting problem, another feature of a voyage that reduces the possibility of a ship going unreported for an unnecessarily long time is simply the number of intermediate ports visited in the course of a passage. There are long ocean passages which ships have the endurance for, but on which there is little margin for safety if fuel runs low, if weather is consistently bad, or if any crisis occurs. Even if equipped with radio, if distances to the nearest ports of refuge are too great, a radio message as well as an emergency deviation to those ports may not be possible. Trans-Pacific voyages, or those from Europe to Australia or to the West Coast of South American are good examples of the long passages required on some such routes.

Probably the best insurance against a ship going missing is the presence of a competent captain and crew. In the case of USS *Cyclops*, the naval collier which in 1918 provided the quintessential disappearance of a modern radio-equipped vessel, the incompetence of the captain, as demonstrated by the consistent over-running of the ship's ports-of-call, appears to have been a major factor in her loss, regardless of the specific cause of the ship's demise.[13]

The specific causes of a ship's disappearance and ultimate loss can obviously take a number of forms. Some are due to human action, and others to natural phenomena. Among the causes attributable to humans, many are unintentional such as poor performance of duty aboard the vessel in the form of sloppy navigation or dangerous engineering practices in leaving slack tanks or open valves which contribute to stability problems. Support staff ashore can also make judgments that lead to the loss of ships in such matters as improper cargo stowage, poor maintenance of the hull, failure to provide current navigational information, etc.

Intentional actions that cause ships to go missing are, of course, more sinister. Aboard ship these might take the form of sabotage, which may seem like a remote possibility in the face of the strong self-preservation instincts of seamen, but in today's world of terrorism cannot be ruled out. Perhaps more likely would be acts that have a profit or control motive such as piracy, barratry, or mutiny; in these actions conspirators hope to take the ship to a secret destination in furtherance of their aims. One has only to check the internet to see how much of this kind of activity continues today.

The most deadly human influences on the disappearance of ships are those that are external and deliberate, coming either from the shore or from other vessels. These are acts of terrorism or war, and include the placing of bombs aboard a vessel before its departure or some kind of attack on a vessel which is designed to sink it. In declared wars, the attacker, with a sense of pride, generally keeps a list of his "kills;" thus, the sinkings are recorded at the end of hostilities when the history of the conflict is written. In World War II German submarines reported their successes regularly by radio, so even if the submarine failed to return from a patrol her results were recorded.

The human motives and frailties which have led to these missing ships are understandable and regrettable. What is equally regrettable but not as readily understood or prevented are the environmental or natural causes responsible for many of these losses. Such an external cause can be regarded under the broad canopy of an "Act of God" which has been defined in admiralty law as "due to natural causes directly and exclusively, without human intervention, and not preventable by any amount of foresight and care reasonably expected of the Master and crew."[14] This explanation of a ship's disappearance, along with its religious overtones of judgment, might cause unease among the survivors of missing crewmen.

Weather is, of course, the major culprit among natural causes. Often in combination with other man-caused circumstances including those in warfare, weather and sea conditions have extracted a heavy toll of ships and men. Most of the ships whose disappearances are recorded in this book encountered some kind of adverse weather which exacerbated their final crisis.

Not only are traditional storms such as gales, hurricanes, and typhoons suspect in the loss of ships, but certain weather phenomena, properly identified for the first time only within the past several decades, should be considered as well. Such things as "rogue" waves, wind-shear, and micro bursts can cause localized effects which may go unnoticed a short distance away. The Oregon coast experienced a well-remembered example in the fall of 1962 when the infamous and largely cloudless "Columbus Day Storm" with top winds measured at 170 miles per hour occurred, an event which proved that narrow bands of brief, violent, and unpredicted weather can and do occur.[15]

Other natural causes are even more esoteric, with new scientific investigations leading to the finding that virtually any kind of natural disaster is likely to occur at some time. These studies, for example, have popularized interest in seismic disturbances that affect the sea. The tsunami, particularly since the great Indonesian disaster of 2005, has made the public conscience aware of a major threat to life at sea and along coastlines. Smaller vessels have been known to be swamped and lost in the gigantic waves leading to a genre of ship disaster movies such as *The Poseidon Adventure.*

Still other forms of seismic disturbance might also be possible. At the turn of the 20th century two schooners off the California coast witnessed a violent explosion of water that lasted about two minutes, after which the sea returned to its normal state. Obviously, some kind of geophysical activity took place on the ocean floor.[16] Such an event could have serious consequences in the relatively shallow water along coastlines where a surprising number of ship disappearances have taken place. Bermuda Triangle devotees cite other forms of ocean floor activity such as natural gas eruptions which might lead to the sinking of ships.

One remaining natural cause is the possibility of some type of extra-terrestrial event. Another west coast schooner, en route to Honolulu at about the same time that the two mentioned above witnessed the eruption of water, was struck by a meteorite.[17] There are other recorded instances of small vessels in the Mediterranean also being hit by meteorites. Judging from the number of recent television documentaries on the impact of meteorites on the earth, and from the fact that more than seventy percent of the planet's surface is ocean, such objects certainly would be more common at sea and some capable of destroying a vessel.

Thus, the possibilities in identifying causes for a ship to vanish from the earth are numerous. It seems likely, too, that multiple causes, particularly combinations of weather and human error, are more common than single events or circumstances in starting the chain of events leading to the disappearance of a ship. Of the eight onetime American vessels whose disappearances will be traced in the chapters that follow, two had been colliers in the United States Navy, two had been Army freighters, and one each had been a non-military collier, a naval fleet tug, a freighter and a tanker. That distribution seems decidedly atypical as a cross-section of the American merchant marine and naval auxiliary service during the forty years that spanned the incidents in this book, but it might indicate the vulnerability to marine hazards facing older ships.

The ex-colliers were a particularly interesting group. It has been argued that coal as a cargo has a negative effect on metal, and thus can over time weaken the steel of a ship's hull. That same suggestion has been made regarding other cargoes carried by ships in this study, including bulk sulphur and sugar.

In the case of sugar, perhaps the most surprising comments to this effect came from the distinguished jurist Learned Hand who took judicial notice of the fact that "Steel vessels which carry sugar cargoes are subject to rapid deterioration, and this danger being well known, required the respondent to take extra precautions to keep the vessel seaworthy."[18] This observation came in an action involving the steamer *Elkton* which had a full cargo of raw sugar when she vanished, leaving the oil slick described earlier.

Fortunately, American passenger ships have, for the most part, been spared the fate of vanishing with all hands. However, there are ships which carried passengers aboard that disappeared, including the U.S. Navy's collier USS *Cyclops* in 1918 which included about eighty passengers among her total of 309 men lost.

In the final analysis what we *know* about a vanished ship, and what we *suspect*, depend on the quality of the information we obtain. Sources of information are always difficult to locate. Logbooks go down with ships, and even finding logs of previous voyages in search of clues can be a serious problem. This difficulty is particularly acute for ships operated by small steamship companies which rarely leave well-organized corporate records when they go out of business. Likewise, seamen tend to scatter, so it is difficult to find former crewmen with knowledge of any problems a ship may have had prior to her final voyage. Offsetting the problem of sources, however, is the growing use of deep diving, recreational as well as commercial, as a means of locating the *corpus delecti* of a ship. Although there are ethical issues remaining with respect to the sanctity of a wreck site, the diving community has brought a valuable new dimension to the resolution of ship mysteries. Even in deep mid-ocean location searches, divers and/or remote-controlled submersibles have made substantial contributions to this relatively new understanding of marine disasters.

Technology on a number of other fronts has also contributed to the resolution of mysteries of the sea, particularly when a wreck has been located, the existence of which could end the "disappeared" status of a vessel. Metallurgy provides useful information about the strength of steels used in shipbuilding; however, it should be noted that metallurgical explanations put forth twenty years ago for the sinking of the *Titanic* have been discredited by the more recent retrieval of actual metal from the wreck. Nevertheless, increased metallurgical knowledge of metal fatigue in older vessels may prove useful in looking at cases of disappearance that are more typical.

Similarly, model basins in naval architecture research centers have been used to test theories of wave behavior and other physical phenomena. Studies in these settings have been carried out on the effects of such natural events as tsunamis or other ocean floor disturbances on the height and speed of destructive waves.

Today a more complete understanding of spontaneous explosions than occurred in the first half of the twentieth century allows the investigator to consider a wider range of possibilities in hypothesizing over the quick disappearance of ships. This knowledge is immediately useful in reviewing almost half of the ships in this study — in particular those which were carrying coal or sulphur, commodities known to be subject to dust explosions, — and allows speculation about still other instances of ship loss.

Technological solutions to the mysteries of ship disappearances have the advantage of being objective and free of
human bias. However, since human performance of duty is
probably the ultimate measure of whether a ship will go missing
or not, the findings of technology may have definite limits in
solving the mysteries of most vanished vessels. From a societal
point of view what is obviously needed is some way to study
human decision-making in crisis, and to minimize the future
impact of poor decisions upon the survivability of ships at sea.
Perhaps, in the future lies the possible use of the "black box," now
associated with reconstructing aircraft disasters, in determining
what has happened to a vanished ship through flotation-sensitive
telemetry.

In each of the cases reviewed in the pages that follow the
clues as to what happened range from the virtually non-existent
to the promising but utterly confusing. Unlike shipwreck stories
which generally have some kind of useful eye-witness accounts,
these disappearances must be reconstructed from the last-known
facts of the ship, often without even an indication of at what
point on the ship's final passage her demise took place.

In concluding this orientation, one thing more may need to
be said about the human dimensions of these stories. From an
ethical point of view it is not clear how deeply historians should
probe into the final moments of men who are about to die. In *The
Cruel Sea* Nicholas Monsarrat introduces the disturbing concept
of the quality of dying: this man has died well, and this man
has not died well. This phrase is not a reference to displaying
the proper stiff upper lip or singing "Rule Britannia" as the ship
goes down, (although the American submarine USS *Pampanito*
in 1944 actually came across a large group of British POW
survivors of the sinking of a Japanese "hellship" in the South
China Sea who were singing "Rule Britannia" and "There'll
Always Be an England" as they bobbed in the swells);[19] rather, it
is an indication that some men had been decent and courageous
in life as well as death, and others had not. Perhaps it is just as
well that the final moments of men aboard a disappearing ship,

except in the rare likelihood of diaries that might survive, have not been recorded in that fashion.

With his limitations and his doubts, the maritime historian can only hope to render some useful interpretations of what seems to have happened, and why it seems to have happened that way. Perhaps this book will be modestly successful if it can address the inexplicable nature of ship disappearances at one or both of these levels.

2

THE CURSE OF
THE COLLIERS

The original intent in writing this book was to devote one chapter to each of several interesting ships that disappeared in the Pacific Ocean during the age of steel hulls and mechanical propulsion. Early on, however, it became clear that such disappearances sometimes *clustered* numerically or geographically for reasons that are not always clear, and that those cluster events might speak louder and more comprehensively than single disappearances in identifying the whys and wherefores of these mysteries.

Consequently, two chapters describe the disappearance of more than one ship under similar circumstances that call out for comparisons. In fact, this opening chapter will describe the strange case of the three merchant colliers that disappeared at the same point off the Washington coast, two of them together in December of 1894 and one in December of 1901 in company with a Canadian naval vessel which also vanished. All four vessels left behind some flotsam, recognizable debris that washed ashore, but they all disappeared as did their nearly two hundred crewmen.

This strange series of events took place off the entrance to the Strait of Juan de Fuca, the deep marine trench between the north coast of Washington and Vancouver Island in British Columbia, through which vessels reach Puget Sound or the inland waterways east of Vancouver Island. This ocean area is also referred to as being off Cape Flattery, the northwestern-most point in the contiguous United States, whose lighthouse stands guard over restless seas which have a reputation for being at times brutal.

The approaches to the Strait of Juan de Fuca have always been a deadly spot for mariners, and the danger is particularly great for outbound ships. The area shares, with the Columbia River entrance on the Oregon coast, the soubriquet *Graveyard of the Pacific.* Unlike most West Coast harbors including the Columbia entrance which are bar ports, the waters off Cape Flattery represent the mouth of a fiord, and consequently are deep and subject to strong and complex wind-driven currents which create a notorious "lee shore" which mariners are taught to respect. It is an unforgiving location, too deep for hand-lead or machine soundings to be of much use during frequent and long periods of low visibility. It is also subject to acoustic dead spots which limit the use of a ship's whistle as a sonar-like means of locating the terrain ashore. Simply put, in bad weather, which is common at Cape Flattery, it is essential — but difficult — to know where you are.

The main characters in this first act of maritime drama were coal-carrying ships that plied an important route between mining ports on the east side of Vancouver Island and the San Francisco Bay area, some seven hundred miles to the south. These ships were owned and/or operated by a cast of remarkable men who used them to further their own flamboyant careers, at time beyond the normal legal and moral limits of seafarers.

Two of the three colliers belonged to a West Coast shipping firm with the unlikely name of Saginaw Steel Steamship Company, whose curious identity and ownership we shall explore shortly. The two that went missing in 1894 were the *Montserrat*, owned privately on the West Coast, and the *Keweenaw*, owned by Saginaw. The 1901 victim was the *Matteawan*, also owned by the Saginaw Steel Steamship Company. The *Matteawan* was acquired by Saginaw in about 1900, well after the loss of the *Keweenaw*, so while those two ships might be described as stable-mates, they were not contemporaries. The fourth victim was a British, rather than Canadian, naval vessel, inasmuch as Canada was still part of the British Empire. This ship, rather nondescript in function, was considerably smaller than the colliers, and described along the lines of a sloop-of-war, or, as comparable to a vessel of a later war, a corvette.

One of the problems in exploring early ship disappearances is the absence of a comprehensive reporting and investigative system. The lack of shipboard radio until about 1910, a surprising lack of journalistic skill in dealing with low-technology steamships, and the ineptitude of governmental regulatory agencies all made it difficult for the public to get quick and accurate accounts of wrecked ships or those that had gone missing.

Historians have had a difficult time balancing fact and fiction in this early reporting. In the case of the colliers at Cape Flattery at the turn of the twentieth century, one monumental volume addresses the ships of that time and place: the *Lewis & Dryden Marine History of the Pacific Northwest*. Written in the style of old subscription histories of the 19th century, the book provides considerable useful information about that world, without being critical of anyone or anything in it.[1]

Another generation of historians, although often drawing on *Lewis & Dryden* in the absence of other sources, has provided a more balanced look at the ships, people, and events at Cape Flattery. The dean of that generation of maritime historians was the late James A. Gibbs who drew on his own background with the Coast Guard and as a marine journalist in creating a series of books on perils of seamen in the Pacific Northwest. These sources, in the form of *Lewis & Dryden* as interpreted by Gibbs, provide some much needed continuity to the story of the missing colliers, as does a monograph on the Saginaw Steel Steamship Company by the grandson of the captain of one of the company ships lost at Cape Flattery.

With that background in mind, it is clear that some of the things that will be said about the three colliers lost at Cape Flattery will be reasonably authoritative, while others will be attributed to the best sources available — with the reader being the ultimate judge. There will be disagreements and contradictions, to be sure, but that is the price to be paid for dealing in times and places well removed from those of today.

Even the hard facts are at times difficult to locate and believe. The two colliers that vanished in 1894 are a case in point. Each of them had such a colorful and adventurous background as to make their final service and its daily dangers in carrying coal from Canada to California a proverbial walk in the park. The *Montserrat* even had the appellation *notorious* assigned to her by journalists.

This ship was built at the Hodgson & Soulsby yard at Blyth in the north of England in 1881, and bore the name of a British island in the Caribbean. Her original owner was the International Company of Mexico, a land development firm trying to market small tracts of land to settlers from its giant holdings on the ocean coastline of Baja California. Very little is known about the ship's early use, but reportedly she was acquired to carry silver ore from Ensenada to West Coast ports in California and Guatemala. However, a newspaper account at the time of her loss in 1894 spoke of her having plied "for some months between San Francisco and San Jose de Guatamala," suggesting that she was not kept fully occupied by cargoes in or out of Ensenada.[2]

Photographs of the *Montserrat* are difficult to find, but an old lithograph in the *Lewis & Dryden Marine History of the Pacific Northwest* shows a rather handsome small ship with a well-deck forward and a long shelter deck carrying all the

The Montserrat *gained notoriety during an early period as a "blackbirder" in transporting Pacific Islanders to work in Central America. Her later collier service became more lethal.* Lewis & Dryden.

way aft to a counter stern. Although she had a triple-expansion reciprocating steam engine, she was also rigged for sail, in a brigantine configuration with square sails forward and a fore-and-aft sail on the after mast.[3]

The land promoters in Baja encountered considerable financial difficulty, and soon were looking for a buyer for their ship. In the late 1880s the company, through T. P. H. Whitelaw, head of a prominent salvage firm in San Francisco, sold the *Montserrat* to a pair of San Francisco shipowners, John Rosenfeld and John L. Howard.[4] These men hired as her captain a well-known mariner, David O. Blackburn, who was also something of an entrepreneur. From this moment began the events that resulted in the adjective "notorious" for the ship, and earned the soubriquet "Lucky" for her captain.

Shipping must have been slow at the time as the *Montserrat*'s owners laid the ship up in Oakland Creek, the resting place for idle merchant ships in San Francisco Bay. Understandably, Capt. Blackburn felt chagrin at this turn of events and chartered the ship from Rosenfeld and Howard, reserving the right to buy her at the end of the year 1889. The owners agreed, with Howard supplying financial backing for the charter.

Capt. David O. Blackburn earned the nickname "Lucky" for his skill in turning a profit on any venture. His luck turned against him at Cape Flattery in 1894. Lewis & Dryden.

Captain Blackburn quickly became one of the most creative ship managers the West Coast had ever seen. Essentially, the *Montserrat* became a collier, but one that was available on short notice for special services. Within a year she was heavily involved in trading in Chile where a revolution was taking place; like the old merchant traders of Clipper Ship days on the China coast, Blackburn bought and sold cargoes as well as shipping space. These cargoes included war supplies, from which he made a great deal of money.

After the crisis in Chile faded in 1892 "Lucky" Blackburn found a new gold mine of revenue for the *Montserrat*: "blackbirding," which was the practice of rounding up Pacific islanders and shipping them off to plantations in Central America to work as indentured laborers. To his credit, the captain used persuasion as the inducement to get these people to sign an indenture agreement, rather than simply kidnapping them as many others did. The British Deputy Commissioner for the Eastern Pacific,

Captain Edward H. M. Davis of HMS *Royalist*, generally spoke well of Blackburn's tactics in the Gilbert Islands, from which the *Montserrat* made several voyages to Central America with human cargoes. Apparently, Blackburn had already recruited about 350 islanders at Marakei when Captain Davis first met up with him, and was hoping to sail soon with a total of 600 islanders.[5]

This passage would be made on a vessel only 220 feet in length, measuring out at 849 gross tons, and would go from about 170 degrees east longitude to 90 degrees west longitude, more than one quarter of the distance around the world. Such a passage was more than 6,000 miles in direct distance, or somewhat more going by way of Hawaii to refuel. It is difficult to imagine what living conditions were like during the three-and-a-half weeks or more of the voyage. No facilities existed for bathing other than rainwater showers, and other sanitary facilities were equally primitive. Thus, while Blackburn may have been one of the more humane "blackbirders," even providing a doctor on board, the experience for the islanders crowded into the holds could not be so described.[6]

Through her entire career the *Montserrat* remained registered as a foreign, rather than an American-flag, ship, and her absence from the pages of *Lloyds' Register* make it difficult to know her status. Several sources identify her as a "Hawaiian ship" or an "American-Hawaiian" vessel, suggesting that she was registered there when those islands were not yet under any governmental structure of the United States.[7] Inasmuch as the ship vanished in 1894, and Hawaii was still a sovereign nation until 1893, the possibility of such registration did exist. Also, Hawaii was a common way-port for blackbirders in the 19th century, so the *Montserrat* may indeed have spent time there, giving her the aura of an Hawaiian ship.

All such questions of nationality may have been resolved at the time of the *Montserrat*'s disappearance in 1894 when the *San Francisco Chronicle* explained that, "The [*Montserrat*], lately registered under the Hawaiian flag, now hails from Nicaragua. Captain. W. L. Merry, the Nicaraguan Consul, has the ship's articles for the trip before the last, but those of the last trip are now on the steamer."[8] The meaning of that term "lately" is not completely clear, particularly in view of the fact that two-and-a-half years earlier, Captain Davis, the Deputy Commissioner for the Western Pacific had reported to Queen Victoria upon his establishment of the British protectorate over the Gilbert Islands in mid-1892 that "I found lying here the Nicaraguan steamer *Montserrat* of Corinto, recruiting labor for Guatemala." However, the only reference to the *Montserrat* in *Lloyds' Register*, that of 1894, indeed shows her registered in Corinto, Nicaragua, and owned by Captain Blackburn.

Blackburn was part owner of the ship, but the other owners were not identified. Among those who may have been part-owners were her earlier owner: the San Francisco investors John Rosenfeld or any of his sons who are identified in the San Francisco city directory as shipping and commission agents and wholesale coal dealers, or John L. Howard, the president of a coal company and a sugar firm as well as manager of the Oregon Improvement Company, a shipping firm in the Pacific Northwest. Another possibility was James Jerome, described by newsmen as the ship's agent and by the city directory as manager of the Saginaw Steel Steamship office in San Francisco. Jerome was a direct link to Saginaw Steel Steamship; while living in that Michigan community, and having invested in locally constructed vessels, he became one of the original investors in the new firm, and moved to San Francisco to serve as its West Coast representative.

Captain Blackburn's other profitable employment with the *Montserrat* was in claiming salvage rights for towing disabled ships into port. Her most famous client was a fellow collier, the *Wellington*. This well-known Canadian ship had been built at Newcastle-on-Tyne in 1883, and operated out of Nanaimo for a number of years. The *Wellington* was famous for her own salvage role in 1884 in towing the passenger steamer *Umatilla* in a sinking condition from her grounding site on the Washington coast to the Canadian port of Esquimalt, and for reversing roles in 1893 in

THE CURSE OF THE COLLIERS 27

being the tow when the *Montserrat* brought the *Wellington* 500 miles to San Francisco from offshore where she had experienced an engine casualty. Later her owners filed a suit against the *Montserrat* charging that the towing fee, $15,000, was excessive, but the appeals court found for Captain Blackburn that the fee, while high, was not exorbitant.[9] In an interesting twist of fate, the *Wellington* went on to become a survivor of the great storm of 1901 in which the *Matteawan* and HMS *Condor* were lost, when the *Wellington*'s captain saved his ship by the simple expedient of turning her about, and returning to sheltered waters.

With this historical background on the *Montserrat* now established it will be useful to provide similar information on the *Keweenaw* before describing their joint disappearances in 1894.

The *Keweenaw*'s background was quite different from that of the *Montserrat*, beginning with her construction in 1891 at the F. W. Wheeler shipyard in West Bay City, Michigan. She was somewhat experimental in that her design included a new double-bottom system filled with ballast water that provided protection when the outer hull was pierced. In appearance she displayed a remarkable resemblance to ocean-going freighters dubbed "Lakers," produced in Great Lakes shipyards during and immediately after World War I.

Even though her first and only owner was Saginaw Steel Steamship which soon did not even operate on the Great Lakes, she was apparently originally designed and built for lake service in that her hull, 270 feet on length, was too long for the 185-foot locks of the Welland Canal at Niagara Falls. Consequently, as a finished ship she was built and launched in a way that permitted her to be disassembled and taken through the Welland Canal in a telescoped condition with the stern section inserted into the forward section. She was then reassembled and entered ocean service.[10]

This process, largely one of rivet removal and replacement, apparently weakened her somewhat, and on her long trip around South America, almost a quarter of a century before the Panama

Built as a Great Lakes ship, and taken apart to reach the ocean, the Keweenaw *became a West Coast collier and was lost at Cape Flattery on the same night as the* Montserrat. Maritime History of the Great Lakes.

Canal was finished, she encountered many difficulties. Engine problems required a stop at Rio de Janeiro, she lost her propeller in the Straits of Magellan and was towed 1000 miles to Coronel, and she put into Valparaiso for extensive repairs.

Here, in October of 1891, she stumbled into an international *cause celebre*. Chile was in the midst of a revolution. To monitor the situation United States naval vessels were sent to various Chilean harbors, and the cruiser USS *Baltimore* had recently arrived in Valparaiso for that purpose. A group of crewmen on liberty from that ship was attacked by a mob, with two men killed and a number of others seriously wounded. Then, according to a semi-official history of the U. S. Navy, "offensive remarks by the Chilean foreign minister aggravate[d] the ensuing crisis so that by December war between the United States appear[ed] quite possible." Eventually, in 1892, after an ultimatum from President Benjamin Harrison, Chile apologized for the incident and paid a $75,000 indemnity to the United States, thus averting war.[11]

The *Keweenaw* played a minor but important role in these events through her captain, William H. Jenkins. He had witnessed the attacks in the streets, and described what he saw to American authorities in Chile as well as to an investigative panel, later in San Francisco. His testimony, coming from a civilian but in support of the facts as the U. S. Navy saw them, did much to assure Navy and State Department personnel that their position was correct.[12]

Another little-known aspect of the *Keweenaw*'s time in Valparaiso is well worth noting. As part of President Benjamin Harrison's letter to Congress of January 25, 1892, the story is told briefly and well:

> Upon information received that Patrick Shields, an Irishman and probably a British subject, but at the time a fireman of the American steamer *Keweenaw*, in the harbor of Valparaiso for repairs, had been subjected to personal injuries in that city, largely by the police, I directed the Attorney-General to cause the evidence of the officers and crew of that vessel to be taken upon its arrival in San Francisco, and that testimony is also herewith transmitted. The brutality and even savagery of the treatment of this poor man by the Chilean police would be incredible if the evidence of Shields was not supported by other direct testimony and by the distressing condition of the man himself when he was finally able to reach his vessel.
>
> The captain of the vessel says: "He came back a wreck, black from his neck to his hips from beating, weak and stupid, and is still in a kind of paralyzed condition, and has never been able to work since." A claim for reparation has been made in behalf of this man, for while he was not a citizen of the United States, the doctrine long held by us, as expressed in the consular regulation is: The principles which are maintained by this Government in regard to the protection, as distinguished from the relief, of seamen are well settled. It is held that the circumstance that the vessel is American is evidence that the seamen on board are such, and in every regularly documented merchant vessel the crew will find their protection in the flag that covers them.[13]

It would be interesting to speculate as to what would have happened if the *Montserrat*, which was never registered as a United States ship although owned by Americans, had been the visiting ship.

Early in 1892, after her crew was thoroughly interrogated by the Navy at Mare Island, the *Keweenaw* was finally ready to begin her service as a collier. Her first assignment was a year-long charter to the Black Diamond Coal Company, one of the

Pacific Coast Company's coal operations. She completed ten months of this charter before being relieved by that company's *Mackinaw*, another of the Great Lakes ships acquired by Saginaw Steel Steamship, after which she ran to Panama briefly before moving into the regular collier run from Nanaimo, B. C., to San Francisco.

Eventually the *Montserrat* and the *Keweenaw*, were both on the regular route between British Columbia and San Francisco. On December 7, 1894 each ship happened to be leaving the Strait of Juan de Fuca at about the same time that evening, the *Montserrat* with a load of coal from Nanaimo on the eastern side of Vancouver Island, and the *Keweenaw* with a similar cargo from Comox, another coal port about seventy miles north of Nanaimo. On that date and at that latitude nightfall comes early, and with darkness came another peril of the night, a rapidly developing storm. Soon the two ships were battling their way into the heavy seas off Cape Flattery, unaware that the storm that had moved into the area would turn into one of the longest and fiercest weather systems to hit the northwest coast in decades.

It is impossible, of course, to describe what happened next to the ships. From this moment forward nothing was heard from them; there was little debris; a medicine chest, imprinted SS *Montserrat* was found in late February of 1895 on the coast of Vancouver Island. Months later wooden debris imprinted separately with either *Montserrat* or *Keweenaw* was found in an Indian village on Queen Charlotte Island, well to the north, suggesting that the two ships had been driven far off course by the fury of the storm.[14]

The newspaper follow-up accounts lacked human interest stories of the type generally evoked by such maritime tragedies, inasmuch as most of the crew seemed to have no family ties to the Pacific Northwest or even to the San Francisco Bay area. Aboard the *Montserrat* the second engineer, E. N. Kallock, was scheduled to be married upon his return to California, and aboard the *Keweenaw* was a young apprentice officer, Edward N. Snow, who was the son of a prominent local merchant, as well as a young second mate, H. G. Jenkins, who was the son of the ship's master, W. H. Jenkins.[15] However, most of the crew on both ships was unknown to the newsmen writing the post-disappearance stories. That was true for the officers and crew of the *Keweenaw*, because they had been recruited on the East Coast, and for the officers of the *Montserrat* who came aboard in a variety of places during her "notorious" days, and for the unlicensed crewmen who had been recruited privately by the ship captain through a well-known boarding house crimp* in San Francisco.

Following this storm at Cape Flattery in 1894 newspaper reports spoke of a total of nine American ships still missing two weeks after the storm began. The two colliers, plus two named sailing ships, and five unnamed vessels were lost. Inasmuch as prominent news sources such as the *New York Times* tended to lose interest in distant stories that dragged on without resolution, it is difficult to determine what the total loss of ships and lives eventually was. Aboard the *Montserrat* the toll was twenty-six crewmen, and perhaps several guest-passengers whom Capt. Blackburn was known to carry with some regularity; on the *Keweenaw* it was thirty-one.

Nationally, press and public disinterest was not the case, however, seven years later when the American collier *Matteawan* and the British naval vessel HMS *Condor* went missing. Perhaps because of the collier's war record, her East Coast service, and her British origins, the *Times* showed considerable interest in her disappearance and an understandable curiosity about how a modern naval vessel could vanish as well.

The *Matteawan* was as unlike the *Montserrat* and *Keweenaw* as those two ships were dissimilar to each other. She was built in 1893 at John Readhead & Sons at South Shields, near Newcastle in Northern England, making her eight years old at the time of her loss.[16] The original owner of the *Matteawan* was the Prince Line,

---

* A crimp is a person who tricks or coerces men into service as seamen or sailors. The action of such a person is similar to shanghaiing, and was widely practiced on San Francisco's Barbary Coast.

Service in the Spanish American War provided the high point in the undistinguished record of the Matteawan. *Her disappearance at Cape Flattery in 1901 seemed a fitting demise.* Website: spanamwar.

affiliated with the Furness Withy steamship empire in England, for which she sailed as the *Asturian Prince,* a name honoring an ancient kingdom of Northwestern Spain.[17] Regardless of her patrician name, however, the ship was ordinary in appearance, performance, and other characteristics. Her only noteworthy features were a tall, raked stack and a clipper bow, both of which that seemed out-of-place on her long iron hull with only one superstructure deck. She was 336 feet long, had a beam of 36 feet, and measured out at 3,300 gross tons. Her speed was a modest ten knots.

She was unsuccessful at everything she tried. In fact, none of her owners even bothered to have her inspected and registered through Lloyds, the prestigious issuer of credentials whose approval affirming quality, seaworthiness, and respectability was generally sought by shipowners. Without that registration, tracing her movements and status through her career, short as it was, has been difficult.

She lasted but two years with the Prince Line before a grounding at Curaçao in the Caribbean took her out of service for repairs. She was refloated by salvage vessels of the firm that would later become Merritt, Chapman & Scott, the dominant East Coast salvage operator, and sold as is. Her hull had been damaged significantly, and apparently she was never a robust ship again. More information about this grounding would be useful as a possible explanation of how the stress to her hull might have served as a precursor to her later disappearance, but such information is not readily available.

Even so, the *Matteawan* was still a relatively young ship, and several sets of owners subsequently tried to fit her into their operations. First was the Hogan family in New York, father Thomas and son Charles, who as the Miami Steamship Company reportedly acquired the ship in 1895 at a low price. They, too, bypassed registration by Lloyds. In addition to reflagging her as an American vessel, that firm's most important contribution was the new name they provided which continued through the remaining six years of her undistinguished existence: the *Matteawan.* That name derives from the town of that name on the Hudson River in New York, a place widely known for its state mental institution.

She enjoyed a brief respite from her dreary anonymity in 1898 when she was chartered by the U. S. Army to serve as a transport in Cuban waters during the Spanish American War. Charles Dana Gibson, in his definitive book on Army transports, reports that the ship's career as a military transport lasted three-and-a-half months at a charter rate of $600 per month, and that she could accommodate thirty-five officers and 720 enlisted men, or 368 mules. In the initial landing at Daquiri in June of 1898 the ship, displaying her Army designation, No. 26, on her hull and using her four boats, successfully landed a regiment of the 20th Infantry and two troops from the 2nd Cavalry, as well as the headquarters detachment of an independent brigade, a total of thirty-two officers and 734 men.[18]

However, during her military service the *Matteawan*'s most newsworthy moment occurred at anchor off Tampa Bay when she was almost run down by the *Yucatan,* a transport in which Theodore Roosevelt's "Rough Riders" were embarked. This near-tragedy took place when the latter ship momentarily lost steering control while maneuvering in the anchorage.[19]

After Army duty the *Matteawan* was put into coastal service in 1899 by Miami Steamship Company, running from New York to Galveston for a subsidiary company named the Lone Star Line. The competition, however, in the form of the Mallory Steamship Company, a major coastwise shipping firm, was too much for her. Soon, according to a classic understatement made by The Red Duster, the British website of the Merchant Navy Association, it was apparent that "the venture was not a success."[20]

The details and timing of the next major re-direction taken by the ship at the turn of the century are rather confusing. She was reportedly sold to a company called Saginaw Steel Steamship Company, although *Lloyds' Register,* with whom she had finally been associated, shows *no* owner for her in 1900. That in itself was not an indication that her ownership was in question, inasmuch as about five per cent of the ships listed in the adjacent pages of that volume had a similar blank in the ownership column.

Her price was $250,000, and her buyers were identified as a group of San Francisco investors. In spite of the company's eastern and midwestern origin and name, a British source which followed up on Prince Line ships properly identified the Saginaw Steel Steamship firm as a West Coast company. That source, however, further indicated that the company was managed by John H. Starin, a New York industrialist and political figure who dabbled in steamboat company operation.[21] To set the record straight, it should be noted that Starin was actually the operator of a large wooden side-wheel excursion steamer on Long Island Sound named the *Matteawan*, and it was this vessel, not the former *Asturian Prince*, with which Starin was most likely to have been associated.[22]

However, both *Lloyds' Register* and the *Blue Book of American Shipping* at the turn of the century indicated that the corporate headquarters of Saginaw Steel Shipping Company was located at 100 Wall Street in New York City. The original owners of the company were Arthur Hill, a prominent lumberman from Saginaw who became president of the company; Frank W.

Wheeler, owner of the shipyard that built the *Keweenaw;* James Jerome, the Saginaw resident who had relocated to California; and Samuel Holmes, the New York ship broker who sold the *Matteawan* for the Hogans in New York. When the company was incorporated in New Jersey in 1890 two more original stockholders came aboard, Charles Hogan of the New York firm, and Daniel W. Briggs of Saginaw.

With its New Jersey charter, and its stockholders largely in the East or Midwest, it is not surprising that the company name was not exactly a household word in West Coast shipping circles, although the *McCurdy Marine History of the Pacific Northwest,* successor to the Lewis and Dryden volume and reasonably reputable for its time, properly refers to the company that owned the *Matteawan* as "the Saginaw Steel Steamship Company."[23] However, during her final year, when she was registered with Lloyds' for the first time, that organization's annual ship directory, the *Register,* shows that Saginaw had owned the collier that was lost in 1894, the *Keweenaw,* but not the *Matteawan* whose ownership, as noted previously, was left blank in the 1900 edition.

In any case, the ship's management arrangements seemed awkward at best. Nevertheless, the *Matteawan* did in fact become a functioning West Coast ship. Sometime after her sale to Saginaw, she made the long journey around Cape Horn into the Pacific Ocean — which for a ten-knot ship probably required almost three months. The *San Francisco Chronicle* reported that she was sold in May of 1899 after her war service, and arrived in San Francisco in September of that year. That timetable would require her putting in her time for Miami Steamship to Galveston quickly and briefly after leaving the Army.

Her passage around South America was not without significant peril, which might affect that projected timetable. While at anchor in the Straits of Magellan a lusty wind storm off the mountains caused her to drag anchor, resulting in costly hull damage which, after divers stopped the leaks, was repaired at Punta Arenas at a cost of $10,000. This second grounding, like the first in the Caribbean, may have had some bearing on her future resiliency to heavy seas.

Once in San Francisco, the *Matteawan* began her brief service as a collier shuttling between the coal docks of Vancouver Island in British Columbia and the growing fuel markets of California, and was soon recognized as one of the largest vessels in this trade. By this time, according to maritime historian Jim Gibbs, James Jerome had acquired two other colliers, the *Mackinaw* and the *Edith* to rebuild his storm-ravaged fleet,[24] but this ownership is not reflected in the *Lloyds' Register.*

Many ships that formerly served on the East Coast made this westward shift of home port, and the newspapers of the Pacific Northwest frequently complained that they were so old and frail they were candidates for the scrapyard. To what extent that criticism applied to the relatively new *Matteawan* remained to be seen, but she did have the legacy of the groundings hanging over her. Another criticism of certain ships by residents of the Pacific Northwest may have applied to the *Matteawan* as well. One well-known holding company, the Pacific Coast Company, was owned in New York, but operated passenger ships and bulk carriers as well as coal mines on the West Coast. Because of its somewhat arrogant absentee ownership practices, this company was often subject to intense dislike along the West Coast.[25] Whether the *Matteawan* was similarly subject to prejudice for her absentee ownership, at least if so perceived because of the curious ties to the East Coast and to Michigan of the company that claimed to own her, also remained to be seen. Perhaps, *indifference* would be a better term for the public reaction to the ship than *dislike*. However, the question may be moot; a collier is remote enough from the daily life of local residents to be of little interest.

On the night in question, an unusual center of heavy and treacherous weather quickly enveloped the Strait of Juan de Fuca and Cape Flattery. The second of December of 1901 was a busy night for outbound shipping, and subsequently for tragedy. The demonic spirits of the surf which resided at Cape Flattery may well have been smiling at the prospect of four victims in one night. While that description of the atmosphere of the fatal moment may be a bit facetious, it was true that no less than four ships tried to buck their way out to sea. These four represented two sets of related vessels. Only two survived; the other two disappeared.

One pair consisted of the Canadian naval vessels, HMS *Condor* and HMS *Warspite*. The first-named ship vanished shortly after exchanging signals with the Cape Flattery Lighthouse and departing for Hawaii, while the latter, somewhat larger, vessel struggled through to the open ocean, during which time she lost to the turbulent waters a major deck gun, the empty mount for which would remind her crew when they arrived in Hawaii of how lucky they had been. On the civilian side of the record, the *Matteawan* conveyed her departure to the lighthouse by speaking (which later meant by radio, but at this early time meant vocally through a megaphone) to the keeper, started down the coast, and disappeared. Shortly thereafter, the Canadian-owned collier *Wellington* under the British flag started out close behind the *Matteawan*, but turned around and came back in to spend the night at the tiny anchorage at Neah Bay on the Washington coast.[26]

With the colliers coming down from Nanaimo and the Canadian men-of-war coming out of Victoria it was either a coincidence or an act of fate that the four ships arrived at about the same time off the Cape Flattery Lighthouse which was used as the point of departure for ships leaving the Strait. After the fierce night of December 2nd the southeast gale continued to blow, and the *Matteawan* was reportedly seen from the lonely Washington shore, one of the few stretches of the West Coast of the United States largely without roads, communities, and life-saving stations. However she soon was lost from the observer's view, and was in time reported as missing.

Apparently the Umatilla Light Ship, down the coast a short distance from Cape Flattery, was blown off station during the storm, but it is impossible to know whether the absence of this important navigational aid contributed in any way to the disappearance of the *Matteawan*. It was in this general area that

Native Americans ashore found debris which was subsequently identified as being from the *Matteawan*. Farther south at Destruction Island Lighthouse, the captain of the lighthouse tender *Manzanita*, W. E. Gregory, saw flashlights apparently signaling from the island during the storm, giving him reason to believe that mariners, possibly from the *Matteawan*, were marooned there.[27] However, no confirmation of this theory came from the lighthouse keeper.

The author Jim Gibbs, the doyen of Northwest Coast shipwreck experts, is perhaps the most knowledgeable writer on the fate of the *Matteawan*. He observes, with classic simplicity:

> There was an old saying in the days of the coal ships that they stuck their noses under after rounding Cape Flattery and never came up until reaching the Golden Gate. At the turn of the century a large fleet of steamers and sailing ships was engaged in the trade. Many of them foundered because their reserve buoyancy was so little, due to overloading. The *Matteawan* may well have been such a victim.[28]

Needless to say, the loss of the *Matteawan* created little media excitement on the West Coast. Only a few of the unlicensed crewmen had family living on the West Coast; most of the crew were relatively unknown because the captain recruited them himself, and kept all the paperwork aboard. It is not clear how American seamen could be in a ship touching at near-foreign ports without having to sign shipping articles in front of a shipping commissioner, but these seamen apparently were not required to do so. Captains had the right to recruit seamen directly for "near foreign" voyages to Canada and the West Indies, bypassing the signing of shipping articles in front of a shipping commissioner.

In terms of public disinterest in this type of ship perhaps a collier projected a different image than most ships, perceived by the public more as a machine rather than as a ship manned by thirty-three human beings. Loaded by gravity through hoist-fed tipples and unloaded by equally impersonal hoist-driven buckets, collier operations visible to the public were indeed mechanical, and it was only when they went to sea, unseen by the public, that colliers appeared to be beehives of human activity.

HMS *Condor* as a naval vessel may have generated more concern about crewmen than did an American merchant ship, at least among Canadians. She was gunboat size, 180 feet in length and small for ocean passages in heavy weather. Even though only two years old she was originally rigged with sails as a barkentine.* This arrangement could have permitted her to rig a staysail or some alternative that could assist her in maintaining her heading, but it would also entail sending crewmen on deck in very dangerous seas.

Inasmuch as she was bound for Hawaii, she would probably have taken an initial great circle course well to the west of the collier's southerly course. Within a few days some of her debris, including a ship's boat, turned up near the village of Ahousat, about eighty miles up the northwest-trending coast of Vancouver Island. At one point there was speculation that HMS *Condor* and the *Matteawan* might have collided and sunk one another, but the debris thought to be from the naval vessel and the debris thought to be from the collier which turned up later on the Washington coast were more than one hundred miles apart, so it seems clear the vessels went down separately.[29]

The death toll on the two ships was almost 175 with the *Matteawan* crew representing thirty-three of that number, and HMS *Condor*'s crew 130 or 140. The variation in the number aboard the man-of-war reflected an unconfirmed report that a last-minute draft of ten men was added to the crew of 130 just before sailing from Victoria.

There would be other ships going down at Cape Flattery, including, just four years after the *Matteawan,* the American passenger ship *Valencia* which lost 117 passengers and crewmen in what is often regarded as the most tragic shipwreck on the approaches to Juan de Fuca. That ship's last desperate hours were witnessed by survivors, however, and by observers on the shore; tragic as it was, that disaster resulted in constructive change.

---

* A sailing vessel of three or more masts, the foremost of which is square rigged and the others fore-and-aft rigged.

After an unprecedented hearing by the federal government, a number of reforms were implemented, including the installation of new lighthouses and lightships, the development of a life-saving station at Neah Bay, and the beginnings of ship-borne radio communication on the West Coast.[30]

However, nothing in the way of progress in disaster response resulted from the disappearance of the *Matteawan* or HMS *Condor*, or from the earlier victims, the *Montserrat* and *Keweenaw*. Their losses only demonstrated that ships could be close to a safe harbor and yet vanish, unseen and sometimes unmourned. What did happen, however, was considerable rethinking of the then-current use of small freighters as colliers, particularly those built on the Great Lakes. In matters of disaster *prevention* rather than *response*, several naval architects observed that such ships could not carry enough ballast to stand up to the buffeting of seas which tended to weaken the hulls on return voyages empty, as well as taxing of engines through severe racing. Eventually, when the U. S. Navy launched a major program of collier construction just prior to World War I it built huge ships, larger than battleships in some cases, although it also kept some of the smaller ships used for that purpose, including one to be encountered in the next chapter.

It would be gratifying if the loss of the colliers at Cape Flattery resulted in safer and more efficient large colliers, but the fact remains that the Navy's new fleet of such vessels had an appalling record: six of the twelve ships built in that program disappeared or died violently. Colliers, it seems, were prone to accidents, including disappearances — size did not assure safety.

3

A Navy Veteran

One of the most bizarre cases of a ship disappearing under a cloud of mystery is that of a former U. S. Navy collier, USS *Alexander.* She was sold by the federal government into a shadowy world of unclear identities and loyalties from which she soon vanished completely.

Her new life as a merchant ship was full of intrigue. Within a year after leaving the U. S. Navy, she was under charter to the German Navy in the early days of World War I and seized as a prize by the British; a year later she was loading a cargo of construction material to be taken to the Far East, a move that was generally regarded as assisting the allied cause. After departing from the Pacific Northwest on this voyage, she was never heard from again.

An obscure series of events preceded the strange demise of the ex-USS *Alexander,* making her story confusing. This was compounded by the circumstances of her final voyage, including two of the common difficulties in tracing or analyzing such passages: the absence of a ship's radio, and the lack of intermediate ports at which the ship's progress could be noted.

The voyage was also complicated by wartime conditions which may have required the ship to deviate from traditional well-traveled sea lanes in order to avoid contact with enemy vessels. The result of these conditions was an image of stealth, unlike that which one might expect in the normal course of a wartime voyage by a ship of a neutral nation.

It was her lack of a clear identity, however, that initially presented the greatest problem in understanding what happened to the ex-USS *Alexander*. None of the nations, organizations, or people involved in her operation during her final few years has shown much interest in explaining their role in that operation. As a result, basic information such as ownership and nationality remain unclear.

All these ingredients, plus a few more, came together when this little-known ship left Puget Sound in 1916. Her name had been changed to the SS *Rio Pasig*, a Philippine ship by registration, but, in keeping with the trustee arrangement that existed between the United States and that island nation, flying the American flag.

How she came to be a Navy collier and then a Philippine ship is an interesting story in itself. She was built as a freighter at the Richardson yard in Stockton in the north of England in 1894. She was 330 feet in overall length, 43 feet wide, and 18 feet deep. She measured 3,384 gross tons, and was powered by a triple-expansion steam engine driving a single screw. As a product of the 19th century, she had few of the amenities which we associate with ships of the 20th century. For example, she burned coal rather than oil for her boilers, she had no radio equipment, and she did not have electric lights.[1]

The ship's original owners, a British firm known as the New Star Blue Line, named her *Atala*. In 1898, at the outset of the Spanish-American War, the United States Navy acquired the ship for $207,000 to help meet a shortage of colliers needed

Shown as a commercial vessel (note funnel markings), the Alexander *was a veteran of the Spanish American War, then sold to a Philippine shipping company, renamed* Rio Pasig, *and was involved in shadowy World War I transactions.* Mariners Museum, Newport News.

for their expanding fleet. In keeping with the policy of naming colliers for figures in ancient mythology or history, the Navy gave her the name USS *Alexander* for the great Greek general who conquered most of the known world before he was thirty.

After serving in Cuban waters she was put in reserve status briefly before being restored to full standing as an operational Navy collier. However, she was never assigned any of the sixteen numbers allocated to such vessels by the Navy, and remained one of a dozen such numberless colliers. Despite lacking that designation, her Navy record, albeit dull, was spotless.

Although a ship of the Naval Auxiliary Service with the civilian manning associated with such vessels, she worked from time to time with units of both the Atlantic and Pacific fleets. For the next decade USS *Alexander* served as a second-cchelon fleet collier, after which she endured another period of lay-up at the Cavite navy yard in the Philippines, reflecting the Navy's diminishing use of coal as fuel. She returned to service in 1911, only to serve out two more years before her final decommissioning was ordered in 1913. The Navy never modernized her to burn oil, a reflection of the low esteem in which colliers and the Naval Auxiliary Service were held, both before and after oil became the fuel of choice.

After de-commissioning she was acquired by the Madrigal Company, a prominent steamship operator, then and now, with headquarters in Manila. Company officials gave her a new name with local significance: *Rio Pasig*, for the river that flows through the city of Manila and into Manila Bay.

In 1914 Madrigal chartered the ship to the German Navy for use as a collier. Under this charter she cleared Manila for Guam with a cargo of 5,000 tons of coal. The original intent was for her to supply the German cruiser squadron which was crossing the Pacific from Tsingtao in North China to the West Coast of South America, but the cruisers were too fast and too far ahead to be overtaken by the slow freighter. Instead, she headed for the German naval base at Pagan Island in the Marianas, an island chain belonging, at that time, to Germany.

However, to the chagrin of the German naval officers awaiting her, she diverted from this second destination, and returned toward the Philippines. There she was seized by a British destroyer off the port of Zamboanga on the island of Mindanao. Ultimately, she was interned in British North Borneo,[2] and her cargo was confiscated.

Confidant that the United States was unlikely to protest her capture, the British nevertheless felt the need to rationalize their action in taking her as a prize of war. The Hague Convention of 1907 was ambivalent on the question of what constituted contraband which neutrals were forbidden to carry in their ships. Food and fuel were classic examples of conditional contraband that was illegal to carry to fighting men but not illegal to carry to civilian populations. Since the *Rio Pasig* had been en route to

Through many years in the U.S. Navy, USS Alexander, *later renamed* Rio Pasig, *was part of the Naval Auxiliary Service, unarmed ships operated like merchant ships. Note the crew under the awning on the forecastle.* National Archives.

Pagan Island which was German territory with a small civilian population, it could easily have been argued that the coal was for their needs, and thus not contraband.[3]

A brief exchange of diplomatic notes occurred in late September, 1914, providing the ship perhaps the only real notoriety of her career, albeit strictly of a legal nature. The French and British objected to her actions as aid to Germany. William Jennings Bryan, the American Secretary of State, had the last word in this exchange, saying that there was no breach of neutrality, and that the United States saw no problem either in the ship carrying coal for the Germans or in the British detaining her for doing so. Moreover, this incident does not seem to have generated any indignation or even much interest within the State Department.

At this point the special status, or, more accurately, lack of status that the *Rio Pasig* was destined to enjoy began to emerge. Early in October, 1914, the British Foreign Office published a list of "Vessels Detained in British Ports or Captured at Sea by His Majesty's Armed Forces."[4] No reference to the *Rio Pasig* appears on this list, nor on a related list of ships whose cargoes were detained. Thus, the first elements of the mystery surrounding the ship appeared shortly after her capture. Other mysterious occurrences would be added during the months ahead, culminating in the publishing of post-war lists of ship casualties which failed to include the *Rio Pasig* on either British or American lists, following her ultimate disappearance in 1916.[5]

Irrespective of any remaining legal questions as to her status as a prize, the ship remained in service in the Pacific. It is not clear, however, whether the ship was re-flagged British, changed crews, or otherwise had any status other than that which she enjoyed previously. The fact that the British did not change her name suggests they may have considered her status as a prize to be temporary, inasmuch as they released her after the coal was confiscated in 1914.[6]

At the time of her disappearance two years later, most news sources referred to her as an American ship. She was clearly identified in the 1916-17 volume of *Lloyds' Register* as belonging to the Madrigal Company of Manila, and as flying the American flag. However, in that same source she is shown to have the international call sign, MCVG, which was British.[7]

All these convoluted details of her activities and legal standing in the early part of World War I are included in this account simply to provide information about the strange set of circumstances that had clouded her status in law, some of which may have indirectly contributed to her imminent disappearance.

According to the San Francisco Marine Exchange, late in 1914 the *Rio Pasig* left Manila for the United States. Once here, in February and March of 1915 she made a voyage from the Pacific Northwest to Vladivostok, and remained in the Far East for several months. Eventually, she returned to Puget Sound late in 1915, and began loading lumber for another trip to the Orient.[8] It is not clear whether the cargo included a deck load of lumber, which is always a factor in the stability and survivability of a vessel.

After loading in Seattle, Tacoma, Victoria, and Port Townsend she departed by way of Nanaimo, British Columbia, often used as an outbound coaling stop, on January 2, 1916.[9] She was bound for Vladivostok, the Pacific terminus of the trans-Siberian Railway, under a charter from the Robert Dollar lumber interests. It was while on this voyage that she disappeared and become the subject of speculation.

The San Francisco shipping publication, *The Guide,* listed as the owner/agent for the *Rio Pasig*'s voyage Frank Waterhouse & Co. This British-born Seattle shipping magnate whose firm bore his name had been one of the pioneers in developing overseas markets for the products of Puget Sound, and one focus of his then-current trading activities was the port of Vladivostok.[10] Thus, additional players in the drama of the freighter began to emerge, as well as additional confusion as to the ownership and nationality of the ship.

Although he exercised management control over the *Rio Pasig* while in Puget Sound, it seems unlikely that Waterhouse had anything to do with the subsequent disappearance of the ship. Acting as the general agent rather than the owner, there would have been no mechanism in place for him to collect insurance or otherwise benefit from the loss of the ship. Yet, within a few months the *Seattle Times* identified the *Rio Pasig*, which by that time had disappeared, as one of the ships of the "Waterhouse fleet," so it is possible he had a monetary interest in her.

The only known facts about insurance on the ship are some quotations which appeared in the *Times* of London. Reinsurance rates on the ship are quoted in a column headed "Guineas, per cent" as ninety, one of the highest rates displayed for a group of a dozen ships, all of which had apparently suffered some type of delay in their current voyages.[11] A story in a Seattle newspaper later reported that marine insurance rates had increased fourfold and could go higher, all because of rumors of a German commerce raider in the Pacific,[12] but that was well after the *Rio Pasig* went missing.

The conditions noted earlier that create difficulty in tracing a ship that has vanished were certainly present as the *Rio Pasig* departed for the long trans-Pacific voyage. Her lack of radio would isolate her, and she would not touch at another port in her crossing (she had spent twenty-seven days in her previous westbound crossing in February and March of 1915). Furthermore, she may have had reason to operate in a covert fashion because she reneged on her coal delivery to the Germans in 1914 at Pagan Island, although she survived the earlier round trip to the Orient in 1915 without reprisals.

She would also be traveling a lonely stretch of ocean where she was unlikely to encounter and speak to another ship. The loneliness of her route was the result of choices that each ship captain undertaking such a voyage makes for his own reasons. The direct great circle course from Puget Sound to Vladivostok goes through the Aleutians into the Bering Sea, and touches the Kamchatka Peninsula, considerably farther north than the great circle route to Japanese ports which stays south of the Aleutians. That latter route, if modified at the end to go between Honshu and Hokkaido, would probably provide the route of choice to Vladivostok for most captains. The official distance tables from Seattle to Vladivostok show the mileage to be 4,210, and from Seattle to Yokohama 4,254, so some type of composite route must have been available to the Russian port.

Because it was winter when the *Rio Pasig* made this voyage, her master, identified only as Captain Arlante, along with most other ship masters on the same route probably planned on staying somewhat farther to the south to achieve better weather. Consequently, each captain's choice might deviate from the established mid-summer route to a different degree. Thus, the loneliness of the route was virtually guaranteed, as were the prospects for heavy weather.

As is often the case with vanishing ships, it is difficult to fix a date when the ship was actually regarded as overdue. The entry for the *Rio Pasig* in *Lloyds' Register* for 1916-17 contains a brief overprint which says, "Missing since 1,16," a date which seems to assume that the ship was known to be missing from a time during the voyage, rather than after the anticipated end of it. Perhaps a more realistic assessment was made on March 28, 1916, when the Marine Exchange of San Francisco noted on the back of its movement card for the ship: "March 28 — Vessel has not arrived. Fear felt for crew of vessel." That card, which did not indicate nationality or ownership, also did not show any subsequent ports after leaving Puget Sound, nor did it indicate *where* the ship failed to arrive.[13]

Lloyds, always on the conservative side, waited until July 28, 1916 in London to post the "British steamer" *Rio Pasig* as officially missing, although the *Times* of London had leaked that decision on June 19th, calling the ship an "American steamer." In the meantime, the speculation in the press and shipping journals about her disappearance took on a curious flavor. Suggestions came from several quarters that the ship was the victim of a submarine or was sunk by a mine.

While both submarine and mine warfare were utilized during World War I, generally such operations took place only in the North Atlantic or Mediterranean. Naval war in the Pacific was fought exclusively with cruisers, gunboats, and surface raiders such as the *Emden, Wolf,* and *Seeadler*, and, except for some early skirmishes around the German base at Tsingtao on the coast of China, was confined to latitudes below 30 degrees north. The suggestion that the *Rio Pasig* encountered a German submarine or raider, or struck a mine, en route from Puget Sound to Vladivostok was scarcely worth considering.

Even the rumor mills were relatively quiet on the subject of submarines in the Pacific, despite the efforts of the German naval attache in the United States to introduce such notions. A story datelined San Francisco and appearing in the *Seattle Times* reported on a warning issued by the U. S. Navy to merchant captains that a German U-boat was operating in the Pacific in April of 1917,[14] the same rumor that caused the spiking of insurance rates after the disappearance of the *Rio Pasig*. However, no corroboration of this story ever appeared.

Earlier, a persistent reference to U-boats came in allegations that the mysterious American gun-running tanker *Maverick* was carrying spare parts for submarines along with weapons in her cargo tanks during her voyage in 1915 from San Diego to the East Indies, and in the uncorroborated claims of a German national picked up in San Francisco who announced that he had been surveying sites on the west coast of Mexico for possible submarine bases.[15] Moreover, San Francisco newspapers ran a strange story early in 1918 about reports of a group of interned German merchant seamen who stole a Dutch submarine at Batavia and took her to sea, but even if there were any truth to this wild tale it would have occurred two years after the disappearance of the *Rio Pasig*.

Weather, of course, was the most likely cause of the non-arrival of a ship in the far North Pacific. The great circle route to Japan can place a ship in some extremely foul weather. Pilot charts for the winter months show northwesterly winds off the Kurile Islands and Hokkaido of force 11 and 12 occurring as much as thirty per cent of the time. Those numbers are the two highest categories on the Beaufort Scale, 11 being a full storm and 12 a hurricane.[16]

During the voyage of the *Rio Pasig* to Vladivostok nothing appeared in shipping journals or newspapers to provide reliable clues as to her progress. What little was said was speculation, and subject to correction or repudiation. Soon everyone became confused. For example, the *San Francisco Guide* referred to Frank Waterhouse as the ship's owner. Then, the *New York Maritime Register* on March 29, calling her a British steamer, noted that she was bound for Vladivostok but "was erroneously reported arrived at the latter port on Feb. 10. The vessel is supposed to be lost, as she had not arrived up to last mail date."

Later, this authoritative publication offered several explanations which were difficult to accept. After reporting in April of 1916 that the *Rio Pasig* carried a cargo of "cotton and other merchandise for the Russian government," in May it claimed that the ship was carrying munitions. Both of these reports were at odds with the widely reported view in Seattle that she had a full cargo of Robert Dollar lumber.

This last cargo report apparently prompted the *Japan Times* in Tokyo to repeat the claim regarding the arms which were aboard, citing "news received in shipping circles in Yokohama yesterday."[17] Clearly, the ship reporting system, both on the West Coast and in New York, was not functioning well at this point; the information it provided lacked attribution, and only further confused the issues.

With so much inaccurate information extant, it becomes impossible to determine the fate of the ship. This is particularly true when one considers the unresolved ambiguity in her basic circumstances, including her ownership, nationality, cargo, insurance coverage, etc. It becomes difficult to know to whom basic questions should be addressed. What nation, through what channel of investigation, would have instituted an inquiry concerning this disappearance? What nation would have benefitted from the ship's non-arrival in Vladivostok? What was the ultimate destination of her lumber cargo, if indeed that was her cargo?

A further gap exists in understanding the physical environment of her final days. When one adds in an utter lack of knowledge of the human dimensions of the *Rio Pasig* — the nature of the captain and the men who sailed the ship, as well as the motivations of Frank Waterhouse — it is clear that her fate may remain beyond reconstruction. What does remain, then, is speculation.

The ship's condition and operating capabilities should be considered suspect. She was twenty-two years old, and was subject to the corrosive ravages of coal cargoes for most of her fifteen-year naval career. She was slow, requiring twenty-seven days for a 4,200 mile trans-Pacific passage, or a speed of 6.5 knots. No longer a collier, she could not dip into her cargo hold for reserve fuel when her bunkers were empty. Bunkers on that type of ship would normally hold perhaps 400 tons at most, and coal consumption would run perhaps twenty-five tons a day. Mathematically, about sixteen days was the maximum time she could stay at sea with that fuel consumption. On that basis, her trips across the Pacific seem impossible to achieve without any reserve fuel.

It is interesting to note that the movement card for the ship, as maintained by the Marine Exchange in San Francisco, in the entry just prior "gone missing," showed the *Rio Pasig* stopped at Honolulu en route to San Francisco on November 24, 1915, with the comment, "put in here today short of fuel." Thus, the ship's difficulty in crossing the Pacific without refueling was a matter of record. How, then, in 1915 and 1916 had she made her two westbound crossings which provided no opportunities for coaling? Carrying additional coal on deck, a stratagem that steamers sometimes utilized in crossing the Pacific, might have been utilized by the captain of the *Rio Pasig*. The final stop at Nanaimo provided an opportunity to load coal on deck without any observers in Seattle knowing about it, but only a few days' additional fuel, at most, could be carried. Furthermore, the coal would be subject to the buffeting of mid-winter seas sloshing on deck, a problem compounded by the ship's relatively shallow depth and corresponding small freeboard in a loaded condition.

One other possibility for additional speculation in this mystery lies in an odd coincidence. Almost as an encore to the strange case of the *Rio Pasig* came a follow-up ship disappearance, that of the seventeen-year-old Japanese-flag steamer *Ide Maru*. This ship departed Puget Sound two months after the *Rio Pasig*; she, too, was bound for Vladivostok, with a cargo that included munitions for the Russian government. Lloyds posted her missing on April 8, 1916, only twelve days after her scheduled arrival in the Russian port, even though the earlier disappearance of the *Rio Pasig* was not posted until July 28,[18] fully six months after her scheduled arrival.

Perhaps Lloyds was a bit premature on the *Ide Maru*. On the Red Duster website of the Merchant Navy Association of the United Kingdom, the *Ide Maru*, formerly and again later the *Cardiganshire* of the Shire Line, is identified today as having been owned by G. Katsuda in Japan from 1916-19, and eventually being scrapped in 1923. Thus, she survived the 1916 voyage, but details of that fact are lacking.

Curiously, the press did not make any connection between the actual disappearances of the *Rio Pasig* and the presumed disappearance of the *Ide Maru*, nor did the submarine story

As the Ide Maru, *the* Cardiganshire *vanished in 1916, then reappeared in time to be scrapped in 1923.* www.photoship.co.uk

resurface. Instead, the media chose to assume weather-induced foundering as the cause of the reported loss of the latter ship. It is not clear *on what date* the *Ide Maru* was found to be still afloat; until that awareness developed, all of this confusion pointed toward the entire *Rio Pasig* story as a case of mistaken identity in which some enemy, probably the Germans, waited for a shipload of munitions which they knew was going to Vladivostok, and sank the wrong ship initially but got it right the second time. But without the second disappearance, speculation had to re-focus on the *Rio Pasig.*

There were indeed German efforts to stop Vladivostok-bound ships the previous year. As part of the German-American conspiracies being orchestrated in San Francisco, several agents, potentially dangerous but more often inept, were sent north to place time bombs aboard the *Hazel Dollar* and other ships loading munitions in Tacoma and Seattle for shipment to Vladivostok.

The captain of the *Kaifuku Maru,* which in 1915 was scheduled to carry a shipment of 622 tons of dynamite under a charter to Frank Waterhouse, was threatened by unnamed agents with the loss of his ship if he sailed with that cargo. A huge explosion of a barge containing those explosives at Seattle on Memorial Day of 1915 was blamed on agents from

San Francisco, but no convictions were obtained.[19] One man, thought to have been aboard the barge, was presumed killed in the blast. Undeterred, the *Kaifuku Maru* subsequently continued her scheduled voyage, *sans* explosives, and made a number of additional voyages between Puget Sound and Vladivostok.

Even though one local newspaper on its editorial page treated the barge explosion lightly, almost as a prank, the blast had a latent capability every bit as dangerous as that of the famous "Black Tom" explosion in New York harbor, engineered by German saboteurs in the summer of 1916. Thus, at that time it seemed reasonable for authorities to believe that the two Vladivostok-bound ships that had apparently in quick succession gone missing early in 1916 might have been victims of the pro-German bomb planters.

Another possibility also became evident, but more slowly. If the *Ide Maru* could reappear after being written off as lost, what was to prevent the *Rio Pasig*, which after leaving the U. S. Navy was covered with as much intrigue as she was rust, from surfacing somewhere else in the world, acquiring a new identity, and sailing for a few more years?

With such new scenarios introduced to an analysis that otherwise has been headed toward an indecisive conclusion, perhaps it is wise to revise that conclusion toward something more positive. Thus, it seems reasonable to conclude either 1) that the *Rio Pasig* disappeared permanently because of weather or, less likely, through hostile action, or 2) that the *Rio Pasig* disappeared voluntarily and may have survived in some unknown location, as a result of machinations within her management or chain-of-command.

Regardless of which of these scenarios, or of any other conceivable scenario, is favored, it seems reasonable to conclude that the ship's disappearance was consistent with the strange behavior she displayed throughout her post-Navy service for whomever it was who actually owned and/or controlled her.

4

A MYSTERY
WITHIN A MYSTERY

Accounts of such legendary disappearances as those of the schooner *Mary Celeste*, the naval collier USS *Cyclops*, and the tanker *Marine Sulphur Queen* are particularly captivating because they leave us wondering how these living, functioning ships and their crews could vanish in such short periods of time.

Perhaps the only scenario more baffling would be that of a ship that survived an extended twilight zone of mystery before disappearing. In such a case, the established daily routine of the ship and her operating circumstances could not be used as a point of departure in trying to reconstruct what had happened to her, simply because that information is unavailable. Such a ship was the tanker *Maverick*.

Along with her famous vanishing counterparts, the *Maverick* was a prosaic workaday ship, but she differed from the others in that before she disappeared she was engaged in shadowy

Mystery enveloped the Maverick *in her final years, for during her last few weeks she emerged from oblivion to re-appear as a ghost ship.* Puget Sound Maritime Historical Society.

activities in distant seas. Early in World War I she was part of a major gun-running operation during which she dropped from sight for more than two years, only to emerge long enough to be reported briefly in the shipping news again before being swallowed up by the vast Pacific Ocean.

The Bermuda Triangle notwithstanding, the vastness of the Pacific makes it an ideal arena for ships to disappear without even being missed for many months. In speaking of the secrecy imparted to the disappearance of ships by various oceans, the novelist Joseph Conrad once said, "The Pacific is the most discreet of live, hot-tempered oceans; the chilly Antarctic can keep a secret, too, but more in the matter of a grave." Echoing that theme, this is the saga of a well-kept secret, the strange disappearance of a ship in the farthest reaches of the Pacific. The story became even more bizarre as distorted and inaccurate news concerning her final days made its way across the largest of oceans.

To compound the mystery, the *Maverick* reappeared as a ghost ship on the opposite side of the Pacific, months after she was believed lost! Officers of no less than three well-known ships witnessed her apparition in confrontations which they perceived to be hostile to their own safety.

The strange tale begins with the construction of the *Maverick* in Baltimore in 1890 as one of the first built-for-the purpose tankers. She was a single-screw steel vessel, only 240 feet in length, 36 feet wide, and 17 feet deep, measuring 1,560 gross tons, with a capacity of 12,000 barrels* of oil in her tanks. Although by today's standards she might be considered small, she was as large as most tankers of that era. Not a handsome ship by any stretch of the imagination, she was nevertheless serviceable and reliable. For seventeen years she worked for the Standard Oil Company on the east coast where her most memorable accomplishment seems to have been in 1899 when she delivered, to Halifax, the first bulk cargo of oil shipped into Canada. In 1906 she was sold to Standard Oil of California. Towing a barge that had been sold in the same transaction, she rounded Cape Horn the next year into the Pacific where she would spend the rest of her career.

She quickly settled into her new routine as a products ship — carrying oil, kerosene, and lubricants from the refinery in San Francisco Bay to ports up and down the coast and to Hawaii. By the start of World War I, however, larger and more efficient tankers were appearing, so Standard Oil of California offered the *Maverick* for sale at a reasonable price.

Early in 1915, a strange set of partners in the San Francisco area happened to be looking for a ship. This group was made up of officials from the German consulate and the local shipping community. The shipping men were a mixed group as well; some of them were German who represented firms of that nationality, and the rest were American, both of German extraction and of other national origins. This incongruous group began working together in the fall of 1914 when they discovered that, because the federal government was so slow in adopting neutrality regulations, it was easy to acquire ships and send cargoes of fuel

---

* A barrel of oil holds 42 gallons.

and food to the German cruiser squadron operating off the west coast of South America. With ample funding from Germany, shipowners made a handsome profit, and, in the absence of any objection from the United States government, it all seemed perfectly legal.

Three such voyages were organized. On the first, the small Mexican-flag freighter *Mazatlan* took a load of coal from San Francisco to Guaymas, Mexico, for the German cruiser *Leipzig* then steaming south to join the cruiser squadron off Chile. This merchant ship was owned by Fred Jebsen, a reserve officer in the German Navy who operated a small fleet of merchant vessels from his San Francisco headquarters; he was one of the most innovative plotters among the cargo conspirators in San Francisco. Additional coal was taken south from Guaymas by the *Marie*, owned by Jebsen's brother, which followed the *Leipzig* to serve as her collier.[1]

The second voyage marked the high-point of German ingenuity and American profiteering. A large German freighter, the *Alexandria*, was bottled up in San Francisco at the start of the war. The German members of the shipping conspiracy did not want to risk capture of this ship by the British if they sent her back to sea, so they conceived the idea of registering the ship as American, and using her to take a large load of coal to the German cruisers. A dummy corporation was created by American shipping executives, and the ship was bought from her German owners with money supplied by the German government through the consulate. She now became the *Sacramento*, flying the American flag. The British objected that the Americans were being hoodwinked, but officials in Washington gave their approval of the transfer and for the transport of the cargo. With several German officers aboard, the ship sailed for South America. Eventually, she fueled the entire German Pacific fleet and a number of auxiliaries at Mas Afuera Island, off the coast of Chile.[2]

This voyage was as successful for the American shipping men as it had been for the German supply officers. The ship, provided by the Germans at no cost to the Americans, earned a fat profit on the voyage. Inasmuch as the United States government did not object, another such venture certainly seemed worth a try. Consequently, a third voyage was organized, using the *Olson and Mahony*, a small American steamer owned by the San Francisco-based company of the same name.[3]

Loaded with coal and a large amount of foodstuffs for the German fleet, the *Olson and Mahony* was ready to sail for Chile when American authorities finally heeded the warnings of the British that this voyage, like the other two, was a means of getting supplies to belligerent ships, something a neutral nation was not supposed to do. The voyage was canceled, and no further attempts were made to send cargoes to the German warships.

As an interim activity while planning their next shipping scheme, the conspirators hired several pro-German men to go to Puget Sound to place bombs aboard American ships which were loading cargoes to be taken to Vladivostock for shipment to the Allied forces in Europe. These sabotage efforts were not particularly effective, although they inadvertently created a barge explosion which confused the local authorities at the time of the *Rio Pasig* affair.

Meanwhile, the conspirators developed a new ploy. Still pleased with how easy it had been to get around the vague interpretations of United States neutrality, the Germans at the consulate went ahead with their next scheme involving the *Maverick*. The consulate served as the west coast headquarters of a secret German naval supply system collectively called the *Etappen*, designed to serve the needs of submarines and surface raiders around the world. The earlier trips to South America by the *Mazatlan* and the *Sacramento* were under the operational control of the *Etappe* in San Francisco (the singular of the German *Etappen*) which had worldwide communication links with German agents in many ports. Overall guidance for the operation of this system came from Germany.

Additional orders came from Berlin, in the form of a plan for the San Francisco unit to work with a new group of conspirators, natives from India, anxious to end British rule in their county. The German foreign office under Arthur Zimmermann determined it would be highly advantageous to aid rebels who could keep the British occupied, thus preventing additional troops from being sent to Europe. This plan generally came to be known as the German-Hindu Conspiracy, although other ethnic and religious groups such as Sikhs and Moslems were also included among the rebels. Getting arms to India through a distribution network based in Java became the next responsibility of the *Etappe* in San Francisco with its many friends in the shipping business.[4]

Again using money supplied by the German government, a company was put together to acquire the *Maverick* from Standard Oil. An elaborate corporate structure of ownership, which changed several times after the initial sale, was utilized to conceal the true owners of the vessel. The Germans also worked out a scheme to get around the suspicions that would be raised if the ship were to load weapons at an American port for a destination in the Far East. This scheme called for a smaller vessel, a sailing ship, to take the arms to Mexico; such a shipment was not illegal, even though a revolution was underway in that country. In Mexican waters the arms would then be transferred to the tanker which would carry them to Java for the next step in the distribution process.

The smaller vessel, a 376-ton three-masted schooner named the *Annie Larsen*, was chartered from her owners to carry the weapons to Mexican waters. She was sent to San Diego to pick up her cargo; surplus Army guns and ammunition, old but still serviceable, which a German representative of the Krupp munitions empire had acquired in the open market. The ten-carload shipment consisted of over 8,000 Springfield rifles of 45/70 caliber, 2,400 obsolete Springfield carbines of the same caliber, 410 Hotchkiss repeating rifles, also of the same caliber, and 500 .45 caliber Colt revolvers. Ammunition included almost three million rounds of rifle ammunition, and 100,000 rounds of .45 caliber. Five thousand cartridge belts completed the shipment.

The schooner Annie Larsen *was a partner with the* Maverick *in a gun-running scheme in World War I, but her inability to transfer the weaponry to the larger ship scuttled the plan.* Puget Sound Maritime Historical Society.

The total weight of the shipment was about 275 tons; the value of the guns and ammunition was estimated at $300,000.[5]

The acquisition of the schooner and the loading of her cargo took considerably less time than the acquisition of the *Maverick*. Consequently, the *Annie Larsen* was ready to sail well before the tanker. The schooner's clearance papers indicated that she was going to the port of Topolobampo on the Gulf of California, with a cargo of weapons. In reality, however, the plan called for the two vessels to rendezvous at Socorro Island, 800 miles off the coast of Mexico, where the weapons, but not the ammunition, would be dunked into the half-filled oil tanks of the *Maverick* as a hiding place. This ship was to cooperate with local authorities en route to the Far East, even to the point of permitting inspections, but if the weapons were discovered the ship was to be scuttled.

Inexplicably, the radio set was removed from the *Maverick*; the *Annie Larsen* had no wireless equipment at all. Thus, once they departed the United States the two vessels were unable to communicate with each other. When it seemed clear that staying in port any longer would only give Mexican authorities more time to react negatively to her planned trip, the *Annie Larsen* was sent out of San Diego early in March, 1915, in the hope that she would avoid any inquisitive Mexican gunboats. That departure proved to be too early, however, creating a domino effect which was eventually to topple the entire scheme.[6]

The schooner arrived at Socorro Island, about 270 miles southwest of Cabo San Lucas at the tip of Baja, on March 18, and began her long wait for the *Maverick*. Unknown to those on board the *Larsen*, the tanker was still in the United States. Because of complicated legal maneuvers required to hide ownership of the vessel, plus time spent in a shipyard for repairs, the tanker did not leave the United States until April 23.

The *Maverick* carried an unusual crew. While the engine department included a mixture of nationalities, a group of Kanakas [Hawaiians] from the German-owned Marshall Islands made up the deck department and five natives of India filled out the steward's department. This latter group was sent along as part of the German-Hindu Conspiracy with the expectation that they would handle much of the distribution of arms in Asia.[7]

By the time the *Maverick* left San Pedro for Socorro Island, the *Annie Larsen* was out of drinking water. After her crew dug three wells on the barren island in a futile attempt to locate more, she departed April 17 for the Mexican mainland to replenish her tanks. At Acapulco, the easiest Mexican port to reach with the prevailing northwesterly winds and coastal currents, the schooner encountered a hostile reception from port authorities; members of the Federalist faction in the Mexican revolution. This hostility grew out of the fact that the cargo was consigned to Topolobampo which was a hotbed of revolutionary activity by the rebel forces of Pancho Villa. Consequently, once the vessel's water supply was replenished it was necessary for the captain of the *Larsen* to get help from the U. S. Navy in getting the local authorities to release the schooner so she could return to Socorro Island.

The captain of the gunboat USS *Yorktown* assured the port authorities that the weapons were not intended for Mexico. This was a curious position for a responsible naval officer to take in that the official papers of the vessel clearly said that the weapons were bound for Topolobampo. This officer indicated later that he suspected the cargo was intended for some military action elsewhere in the world, but he did nothing further to intervene.[8]

After leaving Acapulco on April 28, the *Annie Larsen* tried to return to Socorro Island, but found the prevailing northwesterly winds too strong, and was forced to give up the attempt. She tried to reach an alternative rendezvous island, unnamed in accounts, farther to the west, but failed in this attempt as well. Finally, believing that the timetable was now completely upset, her captain pointed the schooner north along the coast toward the Pacific Northwest, her original home territory where she had worked as a lumber schooner before embarking on a gun-running career. In July at Hoquiam, Washington, the ship was detained by the authorities, and her cargo of weapons was ultimately auctioned off at a fraction of the original cost.

Meanwhile, the *Maverick* waited from April 28 until May 27 at Socorro Island. A navy collier, USS *Nanshan*, which arrived on May 6 brought word to those on board the tanker that the *Larsen* had left Acapulco intending to return to the island; it was this information that kept the *Maverick* waiting as long as she did. The tanker captain revealed to the captain of USS *Nanshan* the whole scheme in which the two vessels were involved, but this naval officer, like the one in Acapulco, did nothing to interfere.[9]

Two British warships, however, were more suspicious. At different times both HMS *Kent* and the Canadian cruiser HMCS *Rainbow* visited the anchorage at Socorro Island and inspected the *Maverick*. Between these visits, the Hindus in the crew burned a large quantity of inflammatory pamphlets designed to stir up rebellion in India. In the absence of any other contraband there was nothing that could be done by the British to detain the tanker.

Finally, the *Maverick* left Socorro Island and steamed north. She put in to several of the alternate island rendezvous sites, found nothing, and went as far north as the border of the United States. While the ship remained in Mexican waters, the captain went ashore by launch in San Diego. From there he called the office of Fred Jebsen in San Francisco for instructions.

Jebsen, however, was not available; aware that things were coming apart for the conspirators and anxious to return to Germany to serve in the Kaiser's navy, he had abandoned the enterprise and was on his way east. The secretary who answered the captain's call explained that the office was closed and Jebsen was gone. She then put the captain in contact with the acting German consul, Baron E. H. von Schack, who directed him to take the ship to Hilo in Hawaii.

At this point, for all practical purposes the entire gun-running effort was dead in the water, and probably should have been called off. But the Germans apparently felt they could salvage something by sending the ship on her original projected voyage across the Pacific. Large quantities of arms were known to have been stashed at various points in the Far East in support of the planned rebellion in India; perhaps they felt that they could use the *Maverick* to deliver these weapons. In any case, with most of her cargo of 10,000 barrels of oil remaining on board — but with no weapons — on May 30 she started toward Hilo as the next port of call in her strange odyssey.

The captain was an elderly Danish-American named H. C. Nelson, but his orders were subject to approval by a supercargo, an owner's representative, placed aboard by Jebsen. This man was a young American named John Starr-Hunt who was educated in German schools in Mexico. Originally, he was to have transferred to the *Annie Larsen* at Socorro Island and keep the schooner in Mexican waters, but the failure of the rendezvous forced him to stay aboard the tanker. Later, he provided American authorities with information about the first year-and-a-half of the *Maverick*'s movements.[10]

At Hilo, officials from the German consulate in Honolulu came aboard with new instructions. En route to the Far East, the ship was to stop at Johnston Island, some 850 miles southwest of Hawaii, apparently in a last try to rendezvous with the *Annie Larsen*. By this time, newspaper accounts were speculating about the purpose of the strange voyage, so new orders specified that even if the schooner were located, no transfer of arms would take place. Nevertheless, the Germans apparently still believed that some good would come of the voyage.

After the brief stop at Johnston Island the ship continued toward her initial destination in the Far East, Java, which was neutral territory inasmuch as the Dutch had not entered the war. From this point on, the voyage acquired an air of mystery. Because the ship took a few days longer to make the trip than her rated speed suggested, there was considerable speculation that she either dropped off or picked up a secret cargo along the way. Police in Java believed she dropped off parts of a submarine at a small island. This idea was not as improbable as it sounds for a ship chandler in San Pedro later testified that the fittings he saw loaded aboard the *Maverick*, apparently as a floor of ballast in her lower tanks, might have been submarine parts.[11] Newspaper stories frequently mentioned submarines in connection with the tanker. One in the San Francisco Bay Area spoke of the captain of another tanker just back from the Far East who reported "that the *Maverick* when intercepted by a British cruiser off the island of Borneo was found to have in her hold a knock-down model of a submarine."[12]

Furthermore, both newspaper accounts and intelligence reports later claimed the ship had 5,000 rifles aboard when she arrived in Java, all of which had to be dumped overboard to avoid capture by the British. However, the first group of crewmen to return to the United States swore that the ship had not stopped anywhere between Johnston Island and Java, and that no such incidents took place.

The *Maverick* arrived in Java in late August, 1915. The local representatives from the *Etappe* in Batavia, after waiting for three weeks for the ship, were unhappy with the delay; they were even angrier when they learned that the ship had no weapons on board. Their mood did not change when they decoded their secret orders which Starr-Hunt handed them; these orders said: "abandon the project, sell or charter the ship for whatever you can get for it, and send the crew home."

This change of plans certainly could have been effected earlier in the summer, without sending the ship to Java where her reputation had preceded her, making her a liability for the local Germans.

In October the Dutch authorities interned the ship at Batavia. Although the *Maverick* was a merchant ship under the flag of the United States, a neutral nation, the Dutch were within their rights because of the ship's apparent links with the war efforts of Germany. No protest was made by the United States. The crew was not physically detained; in fact, by the end of 1915 the first group of crewmen had returned to the United States.

A new captain was sent out to command the ship, permitting Captain Nelson and the supercargo Starr-Hunt to depart for America. Even this simple act of coming home turned into a strange drama; Nelson died in Japan en route, and Starr-Hunt was arrested by the British in Singapore where he soon told the local authorities all he knew about the gun-running venture. Beyond this point, however, there is no written record of what happened to the ship. A number of distorted reports appeared in newspapers, but the real fate of the ship for the next twenty-one months remains unknown.

It seems clear, however, that the new captain, William Kessel, thoroughly botched things up. The Maverick Steamship Company, through a new owner, Harry Hart, a San Francisco ship broker fronting for the Germans, expressed irritation and disappointment to the captain for failing to carry out his instructions during the year-and-a-half he had been in command. These instructions called for him to prepare the ship for a charter to take a cargo of oil from Borneo to England. Apparently, Captain Kessel also incurred several debts against the *Maverick*. During this time the ship deteriorated physically from lack of maintenance.[13]

In a strange and utterly inexplicable turn of events, a San Francisco newspaper ran a story about a captain named Griswold who arrived home from the Far East, announcing that he had been in command of the *Maverick* since she arrived in Batavia. His knowledge of the ship and her circumstances seemed legitimate enough, but there is no record of this man ever serving as captain of the ship. The same is true of a man named Erickson whom an authoritative shipping journal in New York identified as the captain of the ship while in Batavia; although this reference may have been to the chief mate who had signed the articles as O. Erickson. This man does *not* appear to have served as master of the *Maverick*.

Eventually, after the United States entered the war and the market value of American-flag ships increased dramatically, the *Maverick* was sold again. In what appeared to be a perfectly legitimate transaction, she was acquired by a sugar company which intended to use her in the molasses trade. The new owner, the West Indies Sugar and Molasses Corporation of Baltimore, was assisted financially by the federal government which was anxious to get the embarrassing vessel back into legitimate trade. This company dispatched a new captain to Batavia to clear up the mess left by Captain Kessel, and to return the ship to the Western Hemisphere and her new service.[14]

Bearing the title of Marine Superintendent for the sugar company as well as captain of the ship, George MacGoldrick went to Java in mid-1917. There he found the ship stripped of all her gear except for boilers and engines. After paying off indebtedness against the ship of about $43,000, plus a sizeable repair bill to a shipyard and the costs of re-equipping and provisioning her, Captain MacGoldrick finally reclaimed the vessel for her new American owners.

Since none of her original crew was available, the captain was compelled to hire a new crew to bring the ship home. Eventually, after the payment of bonuses and transportation costs as inducements, he assembled a Dutch crew in Java. The *Maverick* left Batavia on July 27, 1917, almost two years after arriving. On August 1, she arrived at Tarakan in northern Borneo where the engineers reported that sixteen tubes in the port boiler were leaking. To effect the necessary repairs, Captain MacGoldrick put in to Manila. There, on August 9, 1917, he wrote a letter to the local Collector of Customs, explaining the circumstances of the ship's presence in the Far East.[15]

Although this letter explained how the ship was prepared to start home, it introduced new mysteries concerning the vessel's purchase by her new owners. MacGoldrick indicated that the sugar company bought the ship while she was on a voyage between San Francisco and Sunderland, England, after which she arrived some six months later at Batavia under Captain Nelson's command with no cargo aboard. Yet, Nelson died a year-and-a-half earlier in Japan, and the ship's owners had criticized Captain Kessel for not carrying out the charter to England. These discrepancies in MacGoldrick's letter probably reflected the fact that there was no one left aboard the ship to provide him with anything but hearsay about her past. Despite several confusing statements, this letter was the last word heard from the ship.

On or about August 15, 1917, the *Maverick* sailed from Manila, apparently bound for Cuba through the Panama Canal. Fragmentary and confusing reports remain concerning the circumstances of this voyage. San Francisco shipping journals picked up neither her departure from Batavia nor from Manila; New York sources listed only her intended departure from Manila for Cuba.

Once at sea, the ship was never heard from again. A New York shipping journal on October 24, 1917, said in a story datelined San Francisco a week earlier:

> Steamer *Maverick* is out 62 days from Manila for Cienfuegos and shipping men are speculating as to her whereabouts. The steamer left Manila about the same time as the transport *Thomas* and the schooner *Irmgard*. Both the *Thomas* and *Irmgard* had to put into Keelung, Formosa, on account of being damaged by a typhoon.

Now the growing mystery of the *Maverick* reached full proportion. What happened to the ship? Was she victim of a typhoon? Tankers, particularly when loaded, generally ride well in heavy seas, and it would seem reasonable to assume that the ship was ballasted with seawater inasmuch as she was starting on a long ocean passage in typhoon season.

A valuable clue to the fate of the *Maverick* may lie in the experience of the transport *Thomas*. This ship left Manila on August 15, bound for San Francisco, with 2,000 American soldiers on board, apparently steaming on a great circle route. Two days later, according to her troop commander, Major General Charles J. Bailey, she ran into a typhoon with winds as high as 100 miles per hour. For four days the ship struggled through the typhoon, encountering the calm weather of the eye of the storm before entering the notorious "dangerous semi-circle" on the far side. Finally on the fifth day, after the weather improved, the ship found herself in shoal water off what was described as "one

In 1916 the transport USAT Thomas *is shown undergoing maintenance and repairs in a floating drydock.* Popular Mechanics.

of the little islands off the north coast of Formosa." The captain, recognizing the danger, backed the engines, but the ship struck a rock before reaching deep water. Her bottom plates forward were buckled and torn, but the flooding was controllable. However, the ship was now too low on coal to make the Pacific crossing, and put back toward Keelung, Formosa, for fuel.[16]

En route, she encountered the San Francisco-bound American schooner, *Irmgard*, which was dangerously close to foundering as a result of the storm. The *Thomas* then towed the schooner 180 miles to Keelung, after which the transport refueled and went on to Nagasaki to have her damage repaired before returning to the United States.

If the *Maverick* left Manila at the same time and on the same initial route as the *Thomas* she would have been somewhat south of the transport when she encountered the storm since she was making for the Panama Canal rather than San Francisco. Inasmuch as both the transport and the schooner actually survived the storm, it is difficult to understand how, barring some freak mishap, an ocean-going tanker would be capable of foundering under the same circumstances.

Furthermore, it is entirely possible that the *Maverick* did not take the same route as the *Thomas*. The Pilot Charts of the Pacific show the standard great circle route from the Philippines to the Panama Canal as making use of San Bernardino Strait at the south end of Luzon rather than Luzon Strait at the north. Had the *Maverick* taken the more southerly route, she would have been well behind the storm when she emerged from the strait, two days after leaving Manila, to begin her ocean passage.

The standard distance tables show the great circle distance from Manila to Panama via Luzon Strait as 9,347 miles, and 9,370 miles via San Bernardino Strait, or 23 miles farther going by way of the latter route. However, if navigators wish to break up the long passage (which would take thirty-nine days for a 10-knot ship!) and/or refuel by stopping in Hawaii, which is roughly half-way across and only a bit off the great circle track, the distance from Manila to Honolulu is actually 102 miles shorter by San Bernardino Strait than by Luzon Strait. Consequently, a case can be made for using either route.

Modern navigators taking advantage of counter currents in the Pacific might choose to utilize a composite track from Manila to Panama, the so-called central route. This departs significantly from the great circle track, but provides for faster speeds. Greater speed is achieved because ships do not have to buck the prevailing west-flowing winds and currents farther north, and actually pick up an east-flowing current of one-half to one knot (which could increase the speed of a 10-knot ship by five to ten per cent). Joining this route via Luzon Strait makes the total distance to Panama about ninety miles farther than doing so by way of San Bernardino Strait. However, navigators of earlier times may not have had this hydrographic information available to them, so their choice of route was more likely to be made from distance tables or personal preference. Thus, it is impossible to know what Captain MacGoldrick had in mind as he lay out his course from Manila.

The tropical storm that formed off Luzon was the second to strike the Philippines within a week. It was first tracked as a storm on the 16th of August when already off the northeast coast of Luzon (that date was by Greenwich Civil Time which would make it the 17th in the Philippines). By noon of the 17th, local time, it had become a typhoon and was headed straight north for Taiwan or Formosa. Moving relatively slowly at less than eight knots, it crossed the open ocean south of Taiwan on the 18th — which is when the *Thomas* received the full force of it — and hit the island that night, picking up speed as it went up the coast before blowing itself out in northern China on the 22nd. The storm was indeed intense, but if the *Maverick* went by way of San Bernardino Strait she would easily have missed it. However, had she gone by Luzon Strait she would have been very close to the center of the storm at midnight as the 18th of August, local time, began.

If one assumes, however, that the *Maverick* did not founder, what could have happened to her? What alternative scenarios exist? No German raider was operating in the area, although the *Wolf* was still capturing ships farther to the south in the Dutch East Indies. One possibility, albeit remote, is that the disappearance of the *Maverick* was staged. However, the captain and crew who started home aboard the vessel do not seem to have been a part of the German-Hindu Conspiracy, nor were they men who had reason to engage in further mischief. Consequently, it seems very unlikely that the ship survived to turn up somewhere else, and no reported sightings at other ports suggest that she did.

Nevertheless, she did show up again, at least in perception if not in reality. According to accounts in San Francisco newspapers, the steamer *Paloona* of the Union Line of New Zealand encountered what her officers reported to be the *Maverick* at sea several months later, only 600 miles from San Francisco. On the night of December 8, 1917, the *Paloona* came across flares and rockets, indicating a ship in distress. When the ship investigated, she discovered the *Maverick* without running lights, her distinctive profile set off against a background of ambient light. After the tanker shone her searchlight at the liner, a violation of maritime law, the captain of the *Paloona*, convinced that he had been tricked by the *Maverick*, put his ship back on her original course and quickly left the area.[17]

The captain's reaction reflected the general feeling that the *Maverick* had become a raider. A San Francisco newspaper reported that "It is believed by many in marine circles that the *Maverick* . . . is lying in wait for some faster vessel which the crew hopes to capture and turn into a second *Seeadler*," the reference being to the famous and successful German raider commanded by Count Felix von Luckner which was active in the Pacific in 1917.[18]

Officers of two other well-known Pacific liners, the *Manoa* and the *Maui* of the Matson Line, also reported having seen the *Maverick* between Hawaii and the mainland at about the same time. The one problem in all three sightings is that these Pacific liners had previously had little, if any, contact with the predominantly coastal *Maverick*. In fact, until World War I the

The crew of the Paloona *identified the* Maverick *in a strange encounter.* www.
photoship.co.uk.

Paloona was a coastal vessel in Australia and New Zealand, the
Manoa was built only a year before the war, and the *Maui* was
built while the *Maverick* was still in Java. Consequently, the
officers of the ships would not really have had a good basis for
recognizing the smaller ship unless they had sailed extensively
for other companies in west coast waters before joining Matson
or the Union Line.

In any case, the *Maverick* evolved beyond being merely a
mystery ship, and was now considered a ghost ship. Newspaper
headlines soon announced that the U. S. Navy at the request of
the Department of Justice was conducting a search for the ship
in the "South Seas." As one might expect, no trace of the ship
was ever found.

To this day, there remains no satisfactory explanation of
the fate of the *Maverick*. Although it is a disturbing thought to
acknowledge that her captain and crew may have been unable to
keep her afloat during the typhoon, that scenario comes closer
to explaining her disappearance than any other theory. Ships do
sink with a troubling frequency in bad weather, despite the skills
of shipbuilders and seamen.

As for the sightings several months later in the eastern Pacific, no one can be sure what the officers of these ships actually saw. Perhaps the *Maverick* did survive the typhoon and slowly made her way across the Pacific without radio contact, only to seek help in a way that frightened the *Paloona* off, after which she sank. Or, perhaps another ship similar in appearance to the *Maverick* was experiencing some kind of difficulty which caused her to transmit signals which were mis-read by the New Zealander. The use of rockets and flares on a vessel has been an official distress signal for many decades, but the illegal use of the searchlight toward a potential rescuer might create the specter of hostility. In any case, regardless of how one chooses to explain it, this final episode furnished enough loose ends to prevent maritime researchers from saying, too soon and too smugly, that they definitely knew what happened to the *Maverick*.

As part of the naval and maritime history of World War I, the disappearance of the *Maverick* counted for very little, which is perhaps why her story remains relatively unknown. But in the unique lore of the sea, few vessels have ever vanished under such peculiar circumstances, a fact that ought to give the ship a greater claim to notoriety than she has previously enjoyed. Indeed, what other ship ever came out of a shadowy existence long enough to create the illusion of vanishing from the face of the earth, only to return briefly to the shadows as a ghostly vessel seemingly bent on haunting ships with which she had no quarrel?

Subsequently, other players in the star-crossed drama of the *Maverick* became victims in their own way. Dozens of the plotters — Germans, Americans, and Hindus — were subsequently fined and/or imprisoned by the United States government for their role in cargo and gun-running conspiracies. The mastermind of much of the intrigue and neutrality manipulation, Fred Jebsen, met an ironic death aboard the German *U-36* on which he was serving when she surfaced to capture an innocent-looking fishing vessel which turned out to be a decoy, a British Q-boat whose guns sank the submarine. The *Annie Larsen* was lost during World War I on a lonely Pacific reef, leaving her passengers and crew dependent for survival on a few crewmen who sailed a small boat six hundred miles to Fanning Island to find help.

In retrospect, the story of the *Maverick* has an unsatisfactory ending, in two respects. The first problem, of course, is the inability of historians to learn what really happened to the ship. The second concern is that the loss of the ship was entirely preventable, as were the deaths of Captain MacGoldrick and the pick-up crew who were perhaps the only completely innocent people whose lives were touched by the *Maverick* over a two-and-a-half year period. The Germans, of course, could have halted the operation at any time after the two vessels missed connections at Socorro Island. But, more important, had the two American naval officers on the coast of Mexico who knew of the real purpose of the gun-running mission exercised stronger authority, the *Maverick* could have been kept in American waters, and the loss of the ship and her crew could have been prevented.

In that case, however, the bizarre story of the disappearing and reappearing ship would not have taken place, and the lore of the sea would have been cheated out of this unusual tale.

5

A NAVAL MYSTERY

O ne of the greatest ocean mysteries of the 20th century was the fate of a fleet tug of the U. S. Navy which vanished with all hands while on a routine peacetime voyage to a new home port. A number of clues to her disappearance existed, but no one knew how to read those clues — and, unfortunately, no one seemed interested.

The year was 1921, a time of frustration for the Navy. Still smarting from the disappearance of the collier USS *Cyclops* with 309 men in 1918, it was now doing battle with Gen. Billy Mitchell of the Army's Air Service who was trying to sink its battleships, literally and figuratively. In the midst of that damage to its reputation and pride, the Navy was forced to deal with the disappearance of this additional ship, USS *Conestoga*.

The Navy's overall response to this situation would have to be called inept at best. However, offsetting that performance was an amazing search effort, organized literally overnight which

Shown in the Hudson River in 1911, USS Cyclops *disappeared in 1918 with a loss of 308 men.* U.S. Navy.

became quite possibly the largest air-sea search ever mounted by any navy. What makes the story so unusual is that neither the disappearance of the ship nor the search for her have ever received any significant attention by naval historians. It may be that the Navy wished to forget the entire episode.[1]

No less than sixty ships took part in the search for the missing vessel, but only a single entry in the Navy's official ship history, the *Dictionary of American Naval Fighting Ships* (*DANFS*) mentions the participation of any of those ships in the search – and that only because one of the search vessels also disappeared, albeit temporarily. Likewise, at least two dozen naval aircraft along with a pioneer lighter-than-air craft aided in the search, but they, too, are ignored in histories of naval aviation.

The subject of the massive search was a rather nondescript fleet tug acquired from commercial sources during World War I at a cost of $315,000 — an inflated sum that would normally buy a small freighter. During that conflict USS *Conestoga*, crewed by Naval Reservists, accumulated a less-than-stellar record while towing and escorting small vessels to the Azores. She also developed a frequent need for repairs, particularly to her boilers; thus, she turned out to be no bargain as a wartime acquisition.[2]

USS Conestoga *disappeared while relocating to Samoa to serve as station ship. Fifty-six officers and crew were lost, the greatest peacetime surface ship disappearance in the U.S. Navy.* National Archives.

In addition, she lacked the quality of being a good "sea boat", the term mariners use to describe a vessel whose design enables her to ride out safely and in tolerable comfort, heavy seas. *Conestoga*'s Atlantic voyages in 1917 and 1918 were wet and risky with sea water in the engine room and in the feedwater tanks, and her radios inoperative much of the time. She frequently needed repairs; during one of her many wartime visits to a shipyard Rear Admiral Nathaniel R. Usher, Commandant of the Third Naval District, was quoted as saying that *Conestoga* was "not fit for sea."

Partially offsetting those faults, however, was perhaps her most redeeming feature: modest fuel consumption. Still, with the Navy's towing needs met largely by the wartime construction of the Indian-class tugs and the "Birdboat" minesweepers (a class of fifty-four minecraft named for birds) which doubled as seagoing tugs, it is difficult to understand why the service retained the vessel after the war.

In 1920, when the standard Navy ship designation system was implemented, *Conestoga* became a fleet tug, was designated AT 54, and became a permanent part of the peacetime Navy. Despite her earlier record, she was assigned more challenging tasks. She was selected as the Navy's station-ship in American Samoa, replacing USS *Fortune*, a vintage tug dating from the Civil War. Late in 1920 *Conestoga* began the long voyage from Chesapeake Bay to the South Seas. Towing a coal barge for delivery in Hawaii, she headed west into the sunset, in more ways than one, taking four officers and fifty-two enlisted men of the regular Navy with her.

For reasons difficult to understand, *Conestoga* never acquired a clear identity among those who worked with her. In spite of bearing a name famous in American history from the covered wagons that traveled in great numbers across the plains, her name was frequently misspelled by the media and by the Navy itself. The service's major file at the National Archives on her disappearance refers to her as a minesweeper, and the cover of her own log book designates her as a "seagoing tug," a generic term which, while not incorrect, ignores both her official classification as a fleet tug and her assigned designation number.

Later, Commander in Chief of the Pacific Fleet, Admiral Hugh Rodman, would repeatedly claim he knew nothing about this vessel and her transfer to his jurisdiction.[3] It is clear, however, that CincPac (Commander in chief, Pacific), as well as the Naval District commands along the route, were notified by CNO, the Chief of Naval Operations, of the voyage of *Conestoga*, the status of the vessel, the designation of Pearl Harbor as her new home port, the barge to be dropped off, and all other details of the ship's projected movements. Those movements basically consisted of a passage from Norfolk through the Panama Canal, and up the Pacific Coast to San Diego and San Francisco.

In spite of this advanced information, CNO, CincPac, and the 11th, 12th, and 14th Naval Districts all lost track of *Conestoga* during her final voyage, and seemed unsure of not only what happened to her but also what to do next. Some of the details of the voyage, although covered in the vessel's logbooks, are still wrapped in mystery. Chief among these is the question of the barge she was towing.

The Chief of Naval Operations, Admiral R. E. Coontz, initially directed that the 110-foot 500-ton coal barge No. 468 should be towed to the 14th Naval District in Hawaii, and that the 5th and the soon-to-be-created 11th Naval District could each use *Conestoga* for any additional vessel towing needed during her long passage. The 5th Naval District in Norfolk was authorized to write the sailing orders for the voyage; the resultant orders specified that the barge was to be delivered to San Diego. That discrepancy set the tone for the entire episode of the tug's disappearance.

The barge was important to the story, because the heavy drag it created could, under the right circumstances, exert enough force to submerge the tug — quickly and permanently. Tugs are particularly vulnerable to capsizing because of their lack of beam and to sinking quickly because of their lack of hull compartmentation. Thus, to a tug, a barge is both a *raison d'etre* and a potential hazard.

After *Conestoga* disappeared, and for the ensuing ninety years, there has been no agreement as to whether she was still towing the barge when she left the West Coast. This analysis will offer a new perspective on the barge question, and on other unresolved issues.

After leaving Mare Island Naval Shipyard in San Francisco Bay on March 25, 1921, *Conestoga* apparently was never seen again. Whether she was heard from again is another matter. Two families of crewmen contacted their congressmen to report that they were told by Navy spokesmen through personal contact in one case and by telegram in the other, that the ship radioed that she lost her barge in a storm, but suffered no casualties to the crew. The Navy replied to the congressmen, categorically denying the existence of those messages while making no effort to explain how they might have come about.[4]

At this point, it may be useful to determine what we do and do not know about the ship and her movements. First are her specifications: built in 1904, her hull was 170 feet in length between perpendiculars, 29 feet in breadth, 16 feet in mean draft, and measured 617 gross tons. She had a triple-expansion reciprocating steam engine fired by coal, driving a single screw with 1,000 indicated horsepower which produced a top speed of 13 knots.

The basic facts of the passage she was undertaking are generally not as precise as are those specifications. For example, we do not know exactly when she originally left Norfolk. A message from OPNAV to the Naval Station in Samoa fixed the date as December 1, 1920, and anticipated a sixty-day passage. However, her logbook shows *Conestoga* to have been at Guantanamo Bay in Cuba on that date. DANFS, in its entry for *Conestoga* uses November 18, 1920, as the Norfolk departure date. Local newspapers in Norfolk contain no listings to verify that date; at that time they carried movement reports for merchant ships but not for naval vessels.

It is not clear if *Conestoga* had an automatic towing engine which would keep a fairly constant tension on the towline. In a photo of her stern taken at San Diego she appears to have only the typical double-cruciform bitt abaft her deckhouse, a fairly standard feature for that size tugboat. Neither is it clear if the towline was manila or wire, although a reported radio message from the ship spoke of cutting the line, an action which could happen quickly with an ax on a manila line and require considerably more time with a cutting torch on wire.

Stops were scheduled at Guantanamo Bay, the Canal Zone, and San Diego, California. Two unscheduled stops were also made: one a diversion from Colon, [Panama] Canal Zone, to the Costa Rican banana and coffee port of Puerto Limon in search of another Navy barge to which she was to deliver a part, and another at Salina Cruz on the Gulf of Tehuantepec on Mexico's west coast to acquire fresh water. Arriving at San Diego on January 7, 1921, she spent about six weeks being readied for the voyage to Samoa. The ship's log indicates that upon arrival the barge was taken by a harbor tug to a coal pier at Point Loma at the entrance to San Diego Bay.[5]

During this time in San Diego the crewmen reportedly looked forward to what they anticipated would be their South Sea island paradise. In reality, Pago Pago on the island of Tutuila in American Samoa is well known for its constant and depressing precipitation, made notorious in Somerset Maugham's famous short story "Rain."[6] Ironically, that story was first published in April, 1921, at the same time *Conestoga* went missing.

From San Diego, the tug was sent on to Mare Island Naval Shipyard near San Francisco where she arrived on February 19, 1921. Several factors strongly suggest that she made this passage without the barge: her log makes no reference to re-acquiring it, she made a ten-knot speed going north which was impossible with a tow, and the fleet tug USS *Koka*, AT 31, was seen in late January leaving San Diego with a coal barge, quite possibly the one brought by *Conestoga*.

The trip north was apparently necessitated by the *Conestoga* needing repair work which could not be accomplished at San Diego. However, log book entries, which often carry an indication of the authority or orders under which a naval ship movement is made, contain no hint of the rationale for this visit, nor does the daily log of the shipyard. Throughout this final voyage of *Conestoga,* logbook entries became terse, so it is difficult to determine what instructions the captain was following and what decisions he made on his own.

A strange explanation of *Conestoga*'s visit to Mare Island appeared in a San Francisco newspaper. The *Examiner* noted that the 12th Naval District headquarters indicated that she was an "unattached ship operating under orders from the Bureau of Navigation, and had merely put into this port for food supplies."[7] That explanation asked the reader to accept the Navy's logic that 1) the tug came in to Mare Island, 400 miles north of San Francisco, which would be well off the track for a passage from San Diego to Honolulu, 2,100 miles to the southwest; that 2) the tug came in after two days at sea for the sole purpose of obtaining food supplies, after she had just spent five weeks at the San Diego Naval Station which had a large center containing a variety of foodstuffs; and 3) she found it necessary to stay five weeks at Mare Island, apparently in replenishing her food supplies.

After sending ashore her most recently completed logbooks, covering November through February, and filling her personnel vacancies *Conestoga* departed Mare Island on March 25, en route to Pearl Harbor. No significant storms were reported between Hawaii and the mainland during the next two weeks, contrary to what alleged radio reports quoted by the newspapers would soon say.

Continuing with the known details of the final voyage, we know that she had a bunker capacity of 286 tons of coal, and that she had to travel about 2,100 nautical miles to reach Pearl Harbor which would translate into a nine-day voyage with no tow, or twelve days with a tow. What we do not know is her daily fuel consumption. However, based on her performance in World War I, we can safely assume that her consumption was modest enough to insure that she had adequate fuel to reach Hawaii within two weeks.

We also know that she was equipped with radio capable of both Morse Code (CW) and voice transmission, and she had a radioman, a newly-arrived third-class petty officer, on board. Consequently, it is natural to conclude that something catastrophic happened to the ship or to her radios which did not allow for distress messages to be sent.

It is also quite apparent that no systematic monitoring of the ship's progress took place. On April 4, 1921, by which date the ship should have arrived in Hawaii if she had no tow, OpNav in Washington, which is the headquarters bureau of the Chief of Naval Operations, asked both CincPac and Com12 (Commander, 12th Naval District) to report the date of the ship's departure from Mare Island. Com12's response was prompt, and cited the March 25 departure. CincPac's reply came a day later, and said cryptically "Commander-in-Chief, Pacific, is informed *Conestoga* now at Pearl Harbor."[8]

A communications meltdown now developed. Apparently no one was concerned that *Conestoga* made no movement report indicating her arrival in the islands. Three weeks later CincPac reported to OpNav that the ship had not yet arrived in Pearl Harbor as previously reported. At this point, the CNO, perhaps assuming searches would now be initiated, replied lamely, "Keep Department [of the Navy] informed as to action taken and developments."

A month after the original inquiry, the CNO again asked Mare Island for the departure date of the *Conestoga,* and was told again it was March 25. On this same date, May 2, the 14th Naval District in Hawaii implemented a search for the missing ship in Hawaiian waters with about a dozen ships and a few aircraft, covering a radius of several hundred miles from Oahu.

Few details are available concerning this early and futile effort. The aircraft involved were identified as four HS2L flying boats; the ships were generally unidentified, but were known to include several submarines of the R-type which had gone to Hawaii after the war in large numbers. The most notable event of the search was the near-loss of the *R-14* while patrolling southwest of the island of Hawaii. She ran out of fuel, which left her with no radio capability; she was then forced to rig sails made of blankets and canvas from bunks. After sailing 100 miles in five days the submarine reached Hilo, and a potential tragedy was averted. Her story is told in the *DANFS* vessel histories; peripheral as it is, it appears to be the only reference in that publication identifying any ship that searched for *Conestoga* in Hawaiian waters or later on the West Coast.[9]

In the meantime, no other search was contemplated. It was now May 18, 1921, six weeks after the *Conestoga* should have arrived at Pearl Harbor. On this day occurred the first major breakthrough in trying to establish what happened to the ship. The SS *Senator,* a venerable coastal passenger ship of the Admiral Line, came across a half-sunken lifeboat along the Mexican coast not far from Cedros Island. The ship's crew brought the boat alongside, photographed it, and removed from its bow a brass letter *C.* In the Navy it was a common practice to identify ship's boats by placing on them such a symbol, the first letter of the ship's name, so it is possible this was one of *Conestoga's* lifeboats.[10]

The *Senator's* captain, N. A. Sohst, reported the find to the Navy through the naval radio station at San Pedro. Apparently no specific instructions for identifying further or preserving the boat were radioed back, so he let the boat drift away as the ship departed the area, assuming it would soon sink and thus no longer be a navigational hazard.

Captain Sohst passed along to the Navy another interesting observation concerning the boat. He reported it was badly battered, suggesting it struck its davits and was not launched in the normal manner. Such a theory conjures up images of a taut towline thrashing about wildly on the after boat deck while the captain tries desperately to maneuver to slacken or cut the towline.

It should be noted that in the Navy, ship's boats are not primarily lifeboats; instead, such warships carry boats to conduct ship's business around harbors. Lifejackets and rafts are the primary survival devices for Navy crews, the assumption being that their ships operate with other ships which can assist in the prompt rescue of men in the water. That assumption becomes invalid, of course, when ships operate alone and out of touch with other units, a fact that was brought home dramatically in the loss of the cruiser *Indianapolis* in the final days of World War II.

Several days later, when the *Senator* arrived in San Francisco, Navy officials took charge of the letter *C* and began the attempt to connect it to *Conestoga*. Soon they were forced to announce that neither the letter *C* nor the number on a small plaque underneath it could be determined definitively to have been from *Conestoga*'s boats. What was needed was a serial number cut into the keel of the boat, an identifying feature not called to Captain Sohst's attention. Nevertheless, the prevailing feeling was that this boat was indeed from the missing fleet tug.

The Navy now sprang into action. The CNO radioed CincPac, directing that "a thorough search be made for USS *Conestoga*" in the area along the Mexican coast near where the *Senator* found the boat. The message was received in late afternoon on May 19, 1921; during the evening hours of the same day aboard the cruiser *Charleston* plans were drawn up for the search force to begin to assemble the following day. Overnight, ships were re-fueled, officers and crews recalled from liberty, and logistic details worked out.

During the next several days dozens of Navy ships steamed from San Diego to the assembly area for the search, 700 miles to the south. The search force, which would sweep westward under the command of *Charleston*, ultimately consisted of two other cruisers and thirty-six destroyers representing six destroyer divisions. A second force would work inshore, searching the coastline and offshore islands of Mexico. This force consisted of the fleet oiler *Kanawha*, the mine-layer *Aroostook* which was serving as a seaplane tender, two destroyers, three "Birdboat" minesweepers, and a submarine chaser. The aviation component of this inshore force consisted of the blimp B-3, twelve F-5-L seaplanes, and four torpedo planes.[11]

While the inshore force poked into the channels and coves of the long Mexican coastline, the sweep force was moved west toward Hawaii. The thirty-nine ships were stationed ten miles apart, and steamed at 15 knots except for periods of darkness when they lay to until dawn. The spacing of these ships may have been unrealistic for finding any vessel which might have been barely awash. Moreover, there was a constant need to close ranks as vessels dropped out of the scouting line; five destroyers departed because of fuel shortages, and two others developed boiler trouble.

Nothing was found. Obviously the search was too late, coming as it did more than six weeks after the non-arrival of *Conestoga* in Hawaii. The only useful accomplishment of the effort was the remarkable speed at which it was organized and got underway, and yet that feat was marred by the confusion and shoddy performance of many of the ships. An unnamed evaluator, treating the entire operation as an exercise to be critiqued, later

The F-5-L seaplane was used in the search for the missing tug. Built by Curtis, the plane, right, is shown at the Naval Air Station, Pensacola. U.S. Navy.

was particularly critical of the communications between ships. This officer noted the common belief in the Navy that ten percent never "get the word," and reported that this tradition was upheld during the search.

Communication was indeed the weak link in the entire *Conestoga* incident, and the ten percent of non-receivers seemed to extend even to the highest levels of the Navy. CincPac sent several messages to CNO, claiming again that he was unaware of the existence of the fleet tug and her mission in Pacific waters. CNO responded with growing impatience, citing the specific earlier messages which had contained that information. In response to CNO's request for the source of the information supplied on April 5 which said that the *Conestoga* was already at Pearl Harbor, CincPac named the Commandant of the 11th Naval District in San Diego as his source.

That command, in turn, explained only that they were in error in making that report, and should have said the ship was *en route* to, not *at*, Pearl Harbor.[12] No one offered an explanation of why CincPac turned to the district commandant in San Diego for current information when the ship had left there in February and in the interim entered the 12th Naval District at San Francisco.

The presence of the lifeboat in Mexican waters, as well as the existence of strong currents toward the southeast, strongly suggest that the *Conestoga* could not have been anywhere close to the southwesterly trackline from San Francisco to Honolulu when she encountered whatever trouble it was that caused her lifeboat to become waterborne. That reality in turn suggests, among other things, that the ship might have had serious navigation problems as a result of human or equipment error.

It is possible that the offshore navigational skills of the four officers of the ship were limited. Only one was a commissioned officer, the captain, forty-one-year-old Ernest Larkin Jones who was a temporary lieutenant and a permanent warrant boatswain. In reconstructing the disappearance of *Conestoga* it is wise to devote some attention to this man. It is not uncommon for a warrant officer or an ex-warrant officer to command a seagoing

Lt. Ernest L. Jones, commanding officer of USS Conestoga. National Archives.

vessel, and the fleet tugs of the Navy have often had such officers in command. However, Jones had limited experience at sea, raising questions about his qualifications. The Navy *Register* for 1921 shows that he had only a year and four months in sea service in his permanent rank of warrant officer (with his service on *Conestoga*, much of which time was spent at the dock, counting for a year of that time), and only four years and seven months at sea in his entire eighteen-and-a-half years of service during which eleven years was spent as an enlisted man.

Two of the other officers were temporary warrant boatswains, one of whom, Harvey H. Reinbold, was designated as navigator as well as executive officer. Any of these three deck officers conceivably might have been an ex-quartermaster, one of several rates which were part of the career path to being a warrant boatswain. The other officer was a permanent warrant machinist. Fortunately, there were also two enlisted quartermasters aboard, a first class and a second class, and this pair probably did the bulk of the navigation work. However, a log entry from the ship's canal transit shows that these men "advanced" the clock one hour while westbound, contrary to the procedure of retarding the clock which is necessary in moving to the next time zone to the west. Other time changes were generally unlogged.

Vessels of that era had relatively simple navigation equipment with which little could go wrong. A magnetic compass, a chronometer, and a sextant, together with the appropriate navigation tables, charts, and a Nautical Almanac, would meet most needs. The magnetic steering compass may have been vulnerable to external influences, but daily compass checks against azimuths of the sun would determine any malfunctioning of the several topside compasses. Similarly, noon observations of the sun for latitude, which can be done even with considerable chronometer error, could show if the vessel's heading at meridian was other than the southwesterly direction in which she should have been going.

While there was gale-force weather in the western Pacific during this time, as well as in the higher latitudes of the eastern Pacific, no such weather was reported in the steamer lanes between the West Coast and Hawaii. Such information regularly appeared in the *Monthly Weather Review*, published by the U. S. Weather Bureau, and included reports from individual ships.

The final clue in the *Conestoga* debacle, like the lifeboat episode, began with promise, but ended with the same type of disappointment that characterized the lifeboat discovery. On

As a troopship the USS Floridian *is shown arriving in New York (note Statue of Liberty off the stern) with returning troops in 1919. She later returned to civilian service in the Pacific with the American-Hawaiian Steamship Co.* U.S. Navy.

June 6, 1921, the SS *Floridian*, a merchant ship which was in the Navy's Cruiser-Transport Force in World War I, while making a passage from the Panama Canal to San Francisco came across what appeared to be the hull of a capsized vessel along the Mexican coast. Not only was the hull about the size of *Conestoga*, but the location was not far from where the *Senator* found the lifeboat.[13]

Again, an interesting exchange of messages took place between CincPac and CNO. The former reported the event to the latter, and ended by saying "Think highly improbable this is wreck of *Conestoga* and shall make no search unless Department so desires." CNO responded quickly with "... search for wreck reported by SS *Floridian*. Department desires wreck located and identified if possible." The most interesting aspect of this exchange was the fact that a new CincPac was now feeling the impatience of CNO; in a scheduled and routine change of command Admiral Edward W. Eberle had replaced Admiral Hugh Rodman as Commander in Chief, Pacific.

Admiral Eberle cited as his reason for thinking it highly improbable that this was *Conestoga* was the fact that no one aboard the *Floridian* reported seeing the screw of the overturned vessel. While this may have indeed diminished the possibility that it was the missing fleet tug, the sighting occurred in late evening when such details might not be apparent. Furthermore, no one seems to have given any thought to the possibility that it may have been the phantom barge which was reported in newspapers and through the families of lost crewmen who reported learning about it through Navy spokesmen. In any case, units of the search force which were dispersing now returned to the Mexican coast to conduct a search, but no trace of the derelict was found.

Ultimately, when nothing else turned up regarding the fate of the ship the Navy was forced to declare the vessel lost, and announce the date of the death of her crewmen. That date was set as June 30, 1921, perhaps in a gesture of generosity that allowed a few extra weeks of pay to accrue to the ship's personnel beyond what would have been a more realistic date for their demise.[14]

After the loss of *Cyclops* in 1918, theories of her loss emerged for decades, but no such speculation has ever been offered regarding *Conestoga*. Whether it was the result of the sheer lack of reliable clues or simply the same disinterest that characterized the original search for her, an absence of curiosity has prevailed.

No subsequent events have impacted on the search for the ship, so it is now appropriate to examine in greater detail the various clues to her fate. Unfortunately, it is impossible to thoroughly evaluate the lifeboat and the hull of the derelict as clues because they were never found again. However, even if they could have been examined by Navy specialists and found to be from *Conestoga*, the mystery would remain almost as great.

One aspect of the disappearance of the *Conestoga* has always seemed strange — the absence of any radio messages during her final peril. Yet there may be an explanation. Many maritime historians, including the author, in writing about the disappearance of ships have encountered a common, indeed almost universal, reluctance of ship captains to report the existence of dangerous circumstances to their superiors ashore, or to the lifesaving establishment. This attitude may reflect the fear of censure for their actions in getting into an *extremis* situation, or their own misplaced confidence that they could handle the situation

One additional set of external circumstances took place related to the disappearance of *Conestoga*; this was the disappearance of two merchant ships at about the same time, the schooner *Carroll A. Deering* and the freighter *Hewitt*. These ships disappeared in close proximity to each other in February 1921, off Cape Hatteras, and a large-scale federal investigation was still taking place for them when *Conestoga* went missing. Many somewhat hysterical theories were offered concerning these ships: that they had been the victims of pirates, mutineers, renegade bolsheviks, or other evil forces, much in the same vein as the wild explanations that were offered concerning the collier USS *Cyclops* three years earlier. Curiously, virtually none of that hysteria carried over to *Conestoga*, perhaps because the media paid so little attention to her compared to the copious purple prose generated in connection with the two merchant ships.

One inquiry, however, from a relative of a lost *Conestoga* crewman mentioned the possibility of a mutiny, prompting Theodore Roosevelt, Jr., acting Secretary of the Navy to reply, "The Department considers as highly unlikely the suggestion that the crew of the *Conestoga* were overpowered by mutinous members and that the ship headed for the gold fields of Siberia." That final detail reflected one of the theories proposed in the 1921 disappearance of the two merchant ships off the East Coast which noted that shortly thereafter a number of ships with their names obliterated were reportedly taken to Vladivostok on Russia's Pacific Coast.

Another inquiry, from a midshipman at the Naval Academy, focused on dissent and danger from ordnance aboard the *Conestoga*, eliciting this response from the Navy's historian, Dudley W. Knox: "There is nothing in the records of this office to show whether or not any dissension existed among the crew, or whether she had inflammable explosive matter on board."

Such dissension on a naval vessel does indeed seem unlikely, but the presence of explosives is another matter. Admiral Rodman as CincPac, in spite of his insistence that he knew nothing of the mission of the tug, reported seeing a secret message indicating that there were mines aboard the *Conestoga*, bound for naval bases on the islands of Tutuila and Guam.

Perhaps future research efforts should be directed at narrowing the mystery of the ship's disappearance by finding the solution to several specific questions that ought to have answers. For example, somewhere within the naval establishment there should be records of radio transmissions that could throw light on whether the *Conestoga* sent messages indicating that she had lost her tow in a storm. Three West Coast newspapers reported the *Conestoga* had done just that, through a radio message that indicated she was forced to cut loose her barge, and that the ship's crew was safe. The *San Francisco Chronicle* on May 13th wrote that this incident happened only a few days after the beginning of the voyage to Hawaii, but on the 21st of that month both the *Los Angeles Times* and the *San Francisco Examiner* said it occurred near the end of the passage, with April 8th identified as the date and 500 miles from Hawaii as the location. If this time and place were accurate, the tug took fifteen days to cover 1,600 miles and might easily be nearly out of coal unless she had a barge containing a coal cargo which she could take advantage of.

In addition, there is evidence from the log of a private research vessel which was 500 miles northeast of Hawaii on April 8th that, after an early morning squall with force 5 winds, the seas were moderate the rest of the day, with overcast skies and force 4 moderate breezes. The barometer was well above 30 inches. While these conditions seem relatively benign, it is difficult to know what they would mean to the vulnerable *Conestoga*, particularly with a tow.

The fate of the barge itself should likewise be verifiable in records of floating equipment. The barge was known to exist at the time the fleet tug left the East Coast; moreover, both her logbook and her time in transit indicate that she was burdened with it all the way to San Diego. However, the tug's speed between San Diego and Mare Island was a strong confirmation that she no longer had a tow.

Thus, it is virtually certain that the barge was left at San Diego; what is not clear is whether the barge towed away by the tug *Koka* was the *YC 468*, and if so, where was it taken? The Fifth Naval District had already changed the original OpNav orders which called for the barge to be taken to Honolulu; in a modification of those orders in mid-November it directed USS *Conestoga* to stop at Guantanamo Bay to pick up equipment for "Fueling Barge #8" and load it "on 500 ton steel coal barge #468 for transfer to San Diego, California." Did the captain of *Conestoga* understand the new instructions to call for dropping off both the barge *and* the equipment for yet another barge at San Diego? Or did he simply drop off his barge to avoid having to tow it to Mare Island for whatever repairs the tug needed?

If the tow was left at San Diego or somewhere else along the way, one would expect a paper trail at least as traceable as that created in acquiring the barge. This trail, however, was confused by the existence of a second barge.

Naval inventory records from 1921 show the existence and the disappearance of possibly two barges that figured in this incident. One was the *YC 468*, the barge that *Conestoga* reportedly towed when she left the East Coast, and the other was the *YC 478* which was reported in those same records as specifically having been lost that year while being towed to Pearl Harbor. Inasmuch as each barge was assigned to the 14th Naval District at Pearl Harbor, it is entirely possible that both were being returned to that command by *Conestoga* in a tandem tow.

That would mean, however, that the tug had re-acquired *YC 468* as well as *YC 478* after leaving Mare Island. That might have occurred by stopping at the Tiburon coaling depot on the way out of San Francisco Bay, a departure that took about six hours, three hours more than a normal passage from Mare Island to the sea buoy. More likely, however, it happened in a second visit to San Diego.

The issue is further confused, however, by the Navy's *Ship's Data,* an annual publication which showed the *YC 468* was converted to the ammunition lighter *YE 36* in 1920 at Pearl Harbor, and that the number 468 was no longer being used for a barge — even though *Conestoga*'s logs show her to be towing a barge with that number.

In March 1958 *All Hands* magazine, published by the Navy's Bureau of Personnel, ran a two-page letters-to-the-editor section in response to an earlier inquiry in which a retired Chief Boatswain's Mate named Sutton asked for help in recalling the name of a fleet tug which disappeared with a *tandem* tow between Hawaii and Samoa. A number of readers, largely former chief petty officers but also including a Rear Admiral, supplied the name of the tug as *Conestoga,* and the location as between Mare Island and Pearl Harbor; no one disagreed with the fact that she had a tow. Obviously pleased with the response, the editor in summing up asked rhetorically "Did she sink? Did one of her tows drag her under?" Thus, the idea of more than one barge seems to exist in naval folklore, if not in fact.

However, the existence of a second barge in a tandem tow is easier to hypothesize than to prove. It is useful to recall that CNO in the original sailing orders gave both the 5th and 11th Naval Districts the option to use *Conestoga* for towing for their own purposes in addition to the ongoing tow of the *YC 468.* Thus, the highest authority in the Navy had authorized and anticipated the doubling up of the tows if the district commands so desired, but no evidence exists that this was done.

In fact, the Navy — even the CNO who ordered *Conestoga* to take *YC 468* to Hawaii — appears to have given up on the existence of any barge after the tug departed San Diego. This attitude prevailed in spite of the lost-tow messages received by next of kin and mentioned in newspaper accounts, and, more important, in spite of the Navy's officially admitted loss of the *YC 478* that year, as acknowledged in *Ship's Data.* If that barge was lost en route to Hawaii, a naval vessel was towing her, and logic points to *Conestoga* as that vessel — with the slim possibility that it might have been the *Koka* instead.

Is it possible, then, that *Conestoga* went back to San Diego from Mare Island, retrieved the tow, and continued toward Hawaii, only to lose the barge or barges en route before some catastrophe befell the ship? This scenario makes it easier for wreckage to reach the Mexican coast than would a direct San

Francisco to Honolulu passage. It also explains the messages about the loss of the tow, as well as the Navy's rigid position, which was apparently correct in the narrowest sense in that the *Conestoga*, having lost the tow, did not have a tow when she met her final fate. Incidentally, the entry in the *DANFS* website for *Conestoga* originally listed San Diego as her port of departure en route to Pearl Harbor, rather than San Francisco, but that has recently been changed to the latter port.

This scenario of an additional stop would require a measure of secrecy to be maintained both by the ship and by the 11th Naval District at San Diego, but such secrecy was already demonstrated. *Conestoga* steamed *largely* in secrecy throughout her voyage, reporting nothing to any naval authority during the long passage; similarly, the naval district was secretive in misleading CincPac and CNO on the location of the vessel, possibly by simply guessing that the tug should be at Pearl Harbor by the date it provided to the higher authorities.

Thirty-eight of the crew were available for this photo, taken in 1921 when Conestoga *called at San Diego.* National Archives.

What is not clear is why the Navy seemed so rigidly opposed to accepting the existence of the tow. This concern seems curious, inasmuch as the culpability of the service in the loss of *Conestoga* is not mitigated by the absence of a tow. The inflexibility of the Navy's position, coupled with the lack of an investigation of the disappearance of *Conestoga*, might suggest a cover-up.

Fifty-six men died in the demise of this unpretentious tugboat. Had that number died in a peacetime submarine loss, or in an accident within the spit-and-polish Navy such as that of the destroyer divisions at Point Arguello in 1923 where twenty-two men aboard seven ships died, the world would have heard about it, and books would continue to chronicle the event.

Although the men of *Conestoga* were humble tugboat sailors, in death they deserved better than they received. The Navy's reluctance to investigate their passing and their story for the broader world audience remains as difficult to understand today as it was in 1921.

6

MID-PACIFIC DISAPPEARANCES

Alan Villiers, quite possibly the most prolific writer of the 20th Century on ships and the sea, observed in 1974 in his final book, *Posted Missing,* that "Ships large or small, under any flag, may still go missing anywhere." This chapter is an affirmation of that belief.

Characterized by a change of pace and direction, it is set off from the other chapters in content and focus. Its scope is broader, in that it deals with three distinctly different vanishing ships, only one of which was under the American flag. Each of these ships went missing in mid-Pacific waters during the decade between 1925 and 1935, a period of peace in most of the world, when neither warfare nor intrigue could serve as a smokescreen for what happened.

The first to vanish was the *Elkton,* a freighter built during World War I for the United States Shipping Board (USSB). She vanished west of Guam en route from the Philippines to the

One of the "1105" type ships built during World War I, the Elkton *disappeared in 1927. This type vessel had a distinctive profile.* Steamship Historical Society of America.

Panama Canal in 1927, shortly after losing radio contact with another ex-USSB ship racing to her aid. Second was the *Asiatic Prince*, a two-year old British freighter en route, in 1928, from Los Angeles to Yokohoma. She disappeared about a third of the way across, leaving only a cryptic SOS message. Finally, there was the *La Crescenta* which went missing in 1934. Begun as a dry cargo ship in 1923, she was converted to a tanker while on the ways, and, once launched, her owners, a one-ship company, consistently spent little on her maintenance. Bound for Osaka with a cargo of California crude oil, she was last heard from about half-way into the crossing.

Fairly accurate positions were reported in radio messages from each ship, but offshore search and rescue was still in its infancy and the only remaining clues were oil slicks. Navy vessels were dispatched to search for the *Elkton* and the *Asiatic Prince;* in the case of the *La Crescenta* no such search was conducted, but that lack of action was offset by a follow-up inquiry that was perhaps more intensive than those for all the other ships in this book, albeit providing little consolation to the families of that ship's missing crewmen.

Aviation developed slowly in the Pacific. Until the late 1930s there were simply no aircraft with the range and ability to provide surveillance of large portions of the Pacific from Hawaii or other island bases. Furthermore, much of the central Pacific was under League of Nations mandates granted to Japan, and thus off-limits to American aircraft that might otherwise refuel there.

These circumstances, coupled with the vastness of the Pacific, provided a huge arena in which the drama of disappearance could play out, abetted by several classic causes of ship disappearances. Initially, it was the *Elkton* that set the tone for the three mid-ocean disappearances. Her experience reiterated an old lesson of the sea, that nothing can be taken for granted simply because a ship has a full cargo and is headed home.

In this case the *Elkton*, built and home-ported in Puget Sound, became in 1927 the center of a puzzling one-dimensional mystery. Her loss represented the kind of story that maritime historians delight in spinning for their readers, yet this event remains relatively unknown, even to avid aficionados of sea stories. Her disappearance was a strange story, full of admirable human qualities of friendship and loyalty, but short on technical requirements such as watertight integrity and stability. It was also a story that spawned equally strange sequels for some of the men and ships involved in searching for her.

The *Elkton* was a product of the shipbuilding program of the U. S. Shipping Board through its construction affiliate, the Emergency Fleet Corporation. Ships built by this federal agency were intended to support the Allied cause in World War I, but most of them were not completed until after the end of that war. Among that large group of latecomers was the *Elkton*, completed at the Skinner and Eddy yard in Seattle in 1919. One of fourteen ships built to the specifications of design number 1105 known as the *Edison* class, she was 412 feet in overall length, 54.5 feet in beam, and 34.5 feet in depth, measuring about 6,340 gross tons.

The Skinner and Eddy yard was a success story of World War I shipbuilding. Following its acquisition of an abandoned Seattle shipyard it quickly became one of the most prolific producers of American ships in that war. About three dozen ships were produced there, three of which, including the *Elkton,* were lost in peacetime shipping accidents. Wisely, management shut down the shipyard when the last ship under the USSB contract was finished, so the firm would not have to compete for work in a post-war economy flooded with ships.

The most distinguishing feature of the 1105 design was the profile of the ship. The midship house was interrupted by a small hatch behind the bridge structure, aft of which was the stack and the balance of the deckhouse. The forward section of the deck-house structure was four decks high, including the bridge, but less than twenty feet in length, producing the effect of a tall, narrow structure rivaling the ship's stack in height and slenderness. Captain Edward C. March, who authored numerous articles on the various types of Shipping Board vessels, said of the 1105s there would "be little question about what they were when sighted."[1]

Significantly, according to Captain March, the 1105s were considered "wet" ships — the term seamen use to denote vessels which commonly ship seas on board when deeply loaded. The unusually deep hull of these ships, together with a relatively low freeboard from deck to water's edge, may have resulted in ex-cess water on deck, requiring greater gutter and scupper capacity at deck edges than was built into them. Whatever the problem, the *Elkton* proved to be the only one of the fourteen ships in her class to be lost.

According to one source, the *Elkton* was on a long half-completed round-trip voyage from New York to China and the Philippines. Although still owned by the Shipping Board, she was home-ported in Seattle and operated by the Admiral Orient Line. Another source, however, indicates that she was operated by Lykes Brothers, a Gulf Coast steamship company. With a crew of thirty-six men, she was commanded by Captain Richard Schnellhardt who at age thirty was serving in his first command at sea. He was a native of Seattle, where his parents still lived near the University of Washington campus.

His ship loaded sugar and coconut oil at the port of Pulu-pandan on the Philippine island of Negros, the last port of call

The Liberator, *circa 1921, as taken from an advertising brochure of the Atlantic, Gulf and Pacific Steamship Corp.* Michael Medwid.

before starting the long trip back to the East Coast of the United States on February 9, 1927.[2] In port at that time was another American freighter, the *Liberator*. Also a Shipping Board vessel but under charter to the Barber Line, she was registered in San Francisco where she was built in the Bethlehem shipyard. As another variation of the basic "West" design*, the *Liberator* was something of a cousin to the *Elkton*.

Before leaving Pulupandan Captain Schnellhardt played a round of golf with old friend and fellow captain, thirty-four-year-old Columbus Darwin Smith of the *Liberator*. The two captains made a good-natured bet over which ship would be first to reach the Panama Canal.

Each man was understandably proud of his vessel. Schnellhardt, of course, was relatively new to the *Elkton* and in the process of learning her idiosyncrasies, but Smith had spent several years on the *Liberator*, and was convinced that his ship was indestructible. Another source of pride and camaraderie to seafarers of that era was having served in World War I. Both Smith and Schnellhardt were Navy veterans; in fact, as an ensign commanding a subchaser, Smith won the Navy Cross at the Battle of Durazzo in the Adriatic Sea. Even Smith's current ship, the *Liberator*, served in the Navy during the immediate post-war period.

Like Alan Villiers, quoted earlier, Smith started his career in sail, but had made the transition to power in the Navy during the

---

* The "West" design was a cluster of similar U.S. Shipping Board designs that lacked the standardization of many of the classes of ships built in Eastern yards such as the Hog Islanders, Submarine Boats, Lakers, *et al*. They had raised forecastles and poop decks, but otherwise were flush-decked.

war. It is not clear how his friendship with Schnellhardt developed, inasmuch as merchant captains have little time for social activities. Incidentally, Smith later spoke of his fellow captain and friend as *Richard* Schnellhardt, but the wire services and newspaper accounts about the *Elkton* all referred to the captain as E. C. Schnellhardt. One other minor discrepancy occurred in the description of the route that the missing ship followed in departing the Philippines. The New York *Maritime Register* indicated that the *Elkton* was to go from Pulupandan to Manila before crossing the Pacific,[3] but other accounts have her starting directly toward home from Pulupandan.

With the *Elkton* in the lead the two ships apparently left the Philippines a day apart, and passed through the Straits of Surigao out into the Pacific on a modified great circle course for the Panama Canal with a scheduled refueling stop in Honolulu. The two captains kept in radio contact for the next several days, an arrangement that provided for an unusually good record of the final hours of the *Elkton.*

The weather quickly deteriorated, and became the focus of the messages between the two ships. An out-of-season typhoon, news of which was updated hourly from Manila, was moving east with the ships. Curiously, however, the U. S. Weather Bureau's *Monthly Weather Review* for February 1927 contains no ship reports on this storm which suggests that there were few ships in the area to provide such information.[4]

On February 17, 1927 Captain Schnellhardt of the *Elkton* reported that his ship was having difficulty with the high seas generated by the storm. Captain Smith tried to assure his friend, now 200 miles ahead of him, that the worst of the typhoon had passed his own position, and that the weather ought to improve shortly. As Smith recalled nearly twenty years later,

> A few moments later I received a garbled message from him giving his position, and then, "Come up and stand by." This shocked me, for I knew Schnellhardt to be the kind of man who wouldn't call for help unless the position was desperate. I headed for him right into the teeth of the typhoon, and it wasn't pleasant. A tremendous

head sea was running and the *Liberator* was virtually awash, but she answered the increased revolutions I called for. At times only the bridge and the top masts were out of water. The sea did everything it could to bury the *Liberator*.[5]

No further communication was received from the *Elkton* by the *Liberator*, or by any other ship or shore station. For the next twenty-four hours Smith drove his ship relentlessly to reach the last reported position of the *Elkton*: latitude 14° 16' N and longitude 136° 36' E, roughly 500 miles west of Guam.

When he arrived at that location Smith found no trace of his friend. As he explained in his ghost-written autobiography in 1945,

> The *Elkton* wasn't there, but there was a huge patch of heavy oil on the surface of the sea. We covered an area of 200 square miles looking for signs of the ship but we never even saw a smashed lifeboat. There was nothing — only that dark ugly patch of oil. The conclusion was inescapable. The *Elkton* had gone down.[6]

Captain Smith's ability to tell a story pointedly and well was enhanced by using a famous war correspondent, Quentin Reynolds, as his co-author and collaborator in his autobiography in 1945. Reynolds was one of the premier reporters in London during the dark days of the Battle of Britain, and probably enjoyed the change of setting, while working with Smith who survived a number of personal encounters with danger during his long and colorful career as a merchant mariner and naval officer.

Smith's conclusion concerning the fate of the *Elkton* was reinforced when four Navy destroyers rendezvoused at the position of the sinking to take up the search. Two of these ships, USS *Stewart*, DD 224, and USS *Paul Jones*, DD 230, were sent from Manila; the other pair, USS *William B. Preston*, DD 344, and USS *Sicard*, DD 346, apparently were already at sea. The Navy vessels were 1,190-ton four-stackers from the same World War I construction program, but none had served during the war. Working an established search pattern, these 314-foot ships of 27,000 horsepower spent four days on site but failed to locate any debris or other sign of the *Elkton*.

USS Stewart *DD-224, shown here on station with the Asiatic Fleet, was one of the ships sent in search of the missing Elkton.* Vallejo Naval and Historic Museum.

The diversion of the equivalent of a full division of destroyers to search for the *Elkton* was certainly an atypical response to the disappearance of a freighter, particularly one with a mundane cargo of sugar. Events a few months later would make Captain Smith of the *Liberator* much better known to naval authorities, but at the time of the *Elkton*'s disappearance he was just another merchant captain trying to help a friend. Thus, there was no special rationale for the length and intensity of the search, unless perhaps Navy officials sensed that, with a fairly accurate position of the missing ship, an intense search was justified because it had a good chance of success.

Ultimately the only tangible clue to the disappearance of the *Elkton* was a lifejacket with the ship's name stenciled on it which washed ashore a year later on a beach on the Philippine island of Samar, north of the Surigao Straits.[7] That incident by itself was not proof of the sinking of the ship, but a lifejacket, unlike a ring buoy which is kept on the open deck where it can float free in heavy seas, is distributed to individual crew members. Thus, the discovery of the lifejacket seemed to suggest the strong possibility that at least someone in the crew prepared to abandon ship.

It is entirely possible that some previously-known defect on the *Elkton* may have contributed to her ultimate loss. After her disappearance Silas B. Axtell, an attorney in New York who specialized in labor cases, ran a notice in seamen's magazines saying that he would be interested in contacting any of the ship's former crewmen who left the ship earlier on the final voyage or had served on the previous voyage.[8]

Axtell was a colleague of famous West Coast labor leader Andrew Furuseth and instrumental in getting the Seamen's Act of 1915 through Congress. During World War I he played a prominent role in the prosecution of two particularly vicious officers on Puget Sound vessels, Captain Adolph "Hellfire" Pedersen of the bark *Puaka,* and Frederick "Fighting" Hansen, mate of the barkentine *Rolph.* According to historian Kay Gibson, "By the mid-twenties, Axtell's activities on behalf of seamen became a thorn in the side of many shipowners, who for some five years attempted, albeit unsuccessfully, to have him disbarred."[9]

It is not known what kind of response Axtell obtained in trying to reach the former crewmen of the *Elkton,* but it is clear that no major litigation developed from the loss of the ship. However, an insurance case developed over the vessel's previous voyage which was the final complete round trip she made to the Philippines. This claim involved damage to cargo. A rusty sounding pipe in a hold ruptured and a tank top leaked as well; as a result, oil saturated some of the cargo of sugar. An appellate court decision written by the distinguished justice Learned Hand ruled that the ship had not been seaworthy in all respects because of these uncorrected defects.

In the reports of this case in books of maritime law Hand's views on the harmful effects of bulk sugar were noted succinctly: "Steel vessels which carry sugar cargoes are subject to rapid deterioration, and this danger being well known, required the respondent to take extra precautions to keep the vessel seaworthy." After citing two legal precedents, the finding goes on to say, "But there is no evidence that any precautions were taken."[10]

This position taken by Justice Hand is known as "judicial notice." In effect, it means that a particular idea is so widely held and established that it becomes a given, rather than a debatable point, in legal deliberations. Today it is difficult to find anything in the literature of hazardous cargo to support this strong position expressed by Justice Hand. Indeed, it would seem that the attorney Axtell, being handed that kind of leverage by a jurist as pre-eminent as Learned Hand, should have been able to put together and win an action against the steamship company, but apparently no such case was even filed. However, there were other legal cases lasting ten more years concerning the complex ownership/management of the ship and her operators, apparently in matters of insurance.

It is not clear if any investigation was made by an outside agency of the sinking of the *Elkton*, or even if there was an agency that would have purview over such an event. Perhaps the Bureau of Marine Inspection and Navigation might have had jurisdiction, but that agency had alienated seamen and their families for decades with its "no survivors, no hearing" attitude. Nor was it readily apparent what aspects of the operation of the ship could be suspect if such an investigation were made. The captain's relatively brief tenure in command might suggest his inexperience was a factor, but it would not be just to make such a judgment without knowing more about the man's career and his behavior in moments of crisis. Thus, the sinking of the *Elkton* remains a riddle, even to this day.

As hinted earlier, the sequels to this story, both to vessels and men, were as interesting as was the disappearance of the ship itself. The *Liberator* and her captain, Columbus D. Smith, went on later that year to discoverer and scuttle a remarkable derelict, a former German U-boat given to Japan at the end of the end of WW I as reparations. Another Shipping Board freighter from the Skinner and Eddy yard in Seattle, the *Elkridge*, sistership to the lost *Elkton*, had come across the derelict a few months earlier,[11] but she had only reported it to the hydrographic office without investigating further.

Captain Smith, a southerner who claimed to be the nephew of the notorious Soapy Smith, the con man of Alaskan fame, went on to an exciting career in the Far East. Sequentially, he

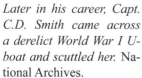

Later in his career, Capt. C.D. Smith came across a derelict World War I U-boat and scuttled her. National Archives.

became captain of a Yangtze River steamer, pilot for the port of Shanghai, commanding officer of the last American naval vessel on the coast of China, prisoner of war of the Japanese, escapee from that captivity, and captain of the port of Shanghai for the Navy.

Subsequently, under another captain the *Liberator* had the unique distinction of having her armed guard crew fire on an American destroyer early in 1942, after which within a few hours she was torpedoed and sunk by a German U-boat. Only four lives were lost in her sinking, but her fabled indestructibility which Captain Smith counted on in driving her through the typhoon-generated seas in search of the *Elkton* proved to be a myth, rather than a legend.

The other conspicuous sequel involved the destroyer *Stewart* which was one of the four naval vessels sent in search of the *Elkton* in the western Pacific. At the start of World War II that vessel was scuttled off her blocks while in a drydock in Sourabaya; she was captured by the Japanese and salvaged, put back into service as a Japanese destroyer, torpedoed and refloated, and ultimately survived the war. The U. S. Navy then opted to sink the ship, and to that end she was brought back to the West Coast where she was bombed and shelled as a target off the Farallon Islands outside San Francisco's Golden Gate.

Thus, the final epilogue involving the players in the *Elkton* saga ended on a strange note of its own, thousands of miles from the original drama that played out in the lonely reaches of the western Pacific. After the passing of these residual components

The least-likely ship to disappear was the Asiatic Prince. *Relatively new, well-built and well-operated, she proved that any ship can vanish.* photoship. co.uk.

of the *Elkton* disappearance, the puzzle of her demise still remains. Likewise, the power of the constructive forces of friendship, tradition, and professional competence — what Conrad may have meant when he said "for all the talk of men — can still not penetrate the mysteries of her loss.

The second ship in this chapter was one of the more difficult to analyze in that she appeared to avoid all the unwise courses of action which might normally put a ship at risk. The *Asiatic Prince*, no relative in bloodline or builder to the *Asturian Prince* which became the collier *Matteawan* before disappearing in 1901 (described in Chapter 2), was relatively new and in good condition. If the broader maritime community were asked to pick a sentimental favorite among these three mid-Pacific vanishing ships, it might easily be the *Asiatic Prince*. She carried in her crew four apprentice officers, earning their sea time to be licensed by the Board of Trade. It was tragic enough that these young men died, but the fact that they were studying under a captain and officers whose actions imperiled the ship made their death doubly difficult to accept.

The Prince Line was one of several steamship companies operating under the general house name of Furness Withy & Company, a giant in British shipping circles, which operated for more than a century before being acquired by Chinese interests in Hong Kong. All Prince Line ships bore an identifying prefix, of a geographical or ethnic nature, followed by the word "Prince" in their name.

The *Asiatic Prince* was the third ship to bear that name for the Prince Line. She was built in 1926 by Deutsche Werft A. G. in Hamburg, one of five identical ships. The Prince Line was occasionally called upon to justify building a ship in a German yard when there were a number of British yards hurting for work, but the company took the position that the German yard simply under-bid the British yards and was awarded the contract solely on that basis.

The *Asiatic Prince* was 441 feet long, the same length as a World War II Liberty ship, with a beam of 60 feet, and measured out at 6,734 gross tons. She was a twin-screw motorship, the only such vessel among the missing ships explored in this book, and had a respectable service speed of 14 knots. A handsome vessel by any standard, she looked more like a product of the 1940s than the 1920s. She had a heavy set of kingposts forward and masts, both fore and aft, and a large and boxy midship house. Her overall appearance was somewhat akin to the American C3-type vessels which appeared just before World War II.

On March 16, 1928, she sailed from San Pedro, California, for Japan, with her port of destination identified variously as Yokohama or Kobe. She had a crew of forty-seven men, including the four apprentices, under the command of Capt. Duncan. That seems a large crew, particularly for a motorship. Unlike steam vessels which require engine room personnel such as firemen and watertenders, as well as coal passers in coal-burning ships, diesel-powered ships can dispense with a number of engine-room ratings. In the improving days of the late 1920s perhaps such savings did not matter to British shipowners to the degree they would a decade later.

Cargo was the important consideration. Aboard she had a special shipment of silver bullion valued at £263,000 or about $1,315,000, along with her regular cargo worth £180,000 or $900,000. The presence of silver would later spawn rumors about her demise.

Six days after leaving the West Coast the *Asiatic Prince* radioed from a position 1,890 nautical miles along her trackline to Japan that she had encountered storms and was reducing speed. On March 24th the British steamship *City of Eastbourne* picked up a faint SOS message whose call letters indicated that she was the *British Hussar*, a tanker not familiar to authorities in Hawaii, rather than from the *Asiatic Prince* which was known to be in the area but was not yet known to be in trouble.

A problem existed in reading the message, which was not sent with the steady hand that one might expect from a sinking ship whose radio operator sensed that he had but one chance to get it right. Radio officers on two other nearby vessels, the passenger ships *Niagara* and *Ventura*, also heard the SOS transmission. They, too, identified the sending station as the *British Hussar.* One of the operators thought he had heard the word "afire" in the indistinct transmission.

The identification problem lay in a single alphabetic letter of the transmission; that letter was the last one in the four-letter code for the sending station. The International Code of Signals, which

The City of Eastbourne *was one of the vessels which heard the faint SOS message sent by the* Asiatic Prince. www.photoship.co.uk.

covered both the procedures for radiotelegraph transmission as well as an extensive set of two and three letter codes for various information and action, also contained four letter codes identifying individual stations, most of which were ships. This code, which incorporated a number of existing practices, was developed at an international conference in 1927 and published in 1931.

In the International Code the first letter of the ship code indicated the nationality of the ship while the other three letters distinguished the ships of that nationality. The call-sign for the *British Hussar,* according to the signal book, was GJVR which is what the operators aboard the three ships believed they heard. The call letters for the *Asiatic Prince* were GJVP, two letters away from that which the three operators heard.

Not only did the two call letters differ only by two adjacent letters, but the International Morse Code symbols for the key letter differed only by a dash. "R" was sent with a dot-dash-dot, and "P" was sent with a dot-dash-dash-dot. Thus the missending of the one letter was responsible for the wrong ship being identified as the vessel in distress.

Authorities ashore knew something was wrong nearby, and contacted Ellerman Line headquarters in London, the owners of the *British Hussar.* There they learned that the company had just heard from that ship which had recently arrived safely in the harbor at Abadan at the head of the Persian Gulf in Iran. It was not until some weeks later, when the *Asiatic Prince* was well overdue in Japan and no other ship reported overdue, that the missing ship in the mid-Pacific was finally identified as the Prince Line vessel. Apparently, even then, Prince Line never connected the *British Hussar* incident with the loss of their ship.

In the meantime the U. S. Navy dispatched several ships — identified as three cruisers in one account, three minesweepers in another, and two named destroyers in a third — to search for the *Asiatic Prince.* But, no trace of her was found. The diversity of these accounts makes it difficult to know what to believe, but perhaps on the matter of this search the versions of the story may not be as far apart as they originally seem. For example, the least traceable reference, that ascribing the search to unnamed cruisers, came from an account in the *New York Times* which followed the story of the missing ship, and probably derived from a wire service story. The account with the three unnamed minesweepers came from a book by the distinguished British maritime writer Alan Villiers, and the one with two named destroyers, USS *Ludlow* and USS *Burnus* (presumably the *Burns*) came from a book by the French mariner-author Robert de La Croix, translated from the French by James Cleugh.

Inasmuch as both USS *Ludlow*, DD 112, and USS *Burns*, DD 171, were converted in the early 1920s to mine *planters*, not *minesweepers,* and both vessels were known to be stationed at Pearl Harbor, it seems reasonable to believe these two ships were the ones mentioned by both Villiers and de La Croix. Both authors seem to be the only maritime historians interested in the *Asiatic Prince*, and their interpretations differ widely, reflecting their backgrounds. Villiers writes in the tradition of Britain's dominance of things maritime and with the expectation that everything should be done in an orderly fashion — "shipshape and Bristol fashion" so named because of the reputed smartness of ships from that port.[12]

On the other hand, de La Croix, identified in his book as a journalist and poet, speaks from his own early experience as a French merchant marine officer, and sees the maritime world as far less orderly and law-abiding.[13]

Somehow public opinion, and that of the maritime industry as well, veered toward the irrational in the wake of the disappearance of the *Asiatic Prince*. The old notion of piracy surfaced and became particularly troublesome; reborn of the *Cyclops* disappearance during World War I, and rekindled by the two merchant ships that disappeared at Cape Hatteras in 1921, it swirled briefly past the *Conestoga* in 1921 before, like a storm, losing its force at sea. Now it seemed to return.

A monograph published in Hong Kong and authored by A. D. Blue later defined the piracy problem in the far western Pacific in terms that supported de La Croix's basic premise that the piracy was of Chinese origin. According to this source, there were fifty-one major cases of piracy on the China coast in the years between the two World Wars. The great majority involved British ships, and twenty British Merchant Navy officers were killed. There were also many Chinese casualties, and many Chinese kidnapped and never heard of again. There were also many cases involving Chinese junks which received little publicity in the foreign press. The worst years were 1922, 1927, and 1928, in which there were five, six, and eight piracies respectively.

The *Asiatic Prince* disappeared in 1928. Compare the reaction of the two authors, Villiers and de La Croix, on the fate of the ship. When he observed that speculation about the fate of the *Asiatic Prince* had taken a strange twist toward Chinese piracy and other fanciful explanations of her demise, Villiers observed:

> She was alleged to be carrying bullion, secret weapons and so forth, and it was even suggested by the wilder theorists that a crew of pirates had managed to get aboard her in Los Angeles before she left (or in China: geography didn't bother these theorists much.) and these had later seized the ship for her gold. . . .

Villiers digressed to scoff at the theories about meteorites or other extraterrestrial sources that might have sunk the ship without any opportunity for her to report. He then returned to his anti-piratical tirade.

> The favorite story was the one about the pirates and, from time to time, that is still brought forward. The *Asiatic Prince*, according to the latest version of the yarn, was lost somewhere in the China Seas, not off the Hawaiian Islands, and the faint radio message received from her contained one decipherable word. The word was "pirates." No such message was received and the ship was not anywhere near the China Sea.

De La Croix differed, however. In his book, written prior to that of Villiers and thus likely the target of the famous mariner's wrath, he had concluded:

What had happened? Simply this. In the middle of the twentieth century a ship had been captured by pirates — Chinese pirates. . . . Their first objective would be the wireless cabin, in order to insure that the operator would not have time to send out distress signals. They would next storm the bridge, so as to force the officers to steer for Bias Bay.

Bias Bay was the infamous home of pirates on the China Coast, located not far from Hong Kong. De La Croix went on to make his point that piracy in the western Pacific was indeed real.

Typical cases were those of the Danish ship *Gustaf Diederichen,* with forty-nine passengers aboard, who were robbed and then left to their fate; the British *Helicon,* which got the better of the pirates in 1930 but not in 1934; another British vessel named the *Angling*; the Norwegian steamer *Prominent,* with eighty-nine passengers; and some years previously the famous *Sunning. . .* In her case the crew were able to put up a fight and succeeded in taking the pirates prisoners. . . . Finally, there was the *Haiching . . .* In December, 1929, she performed a similar exploit, and was eventually rescued by the British cruiser HMS *Bluebell.*

De La Croix had indeed made a good case for the existence of piracy in the 1920s. There were more than a few British citizens and even Americans who agreed. The *Yangtze River Patroller,* the newsletter of a group of old U. S. Navy China hands, several years ago carried a story about the wife of an American naval officer in the 1930s traveling between Shanghai and Chefoo on a British ship with British marines embarked to prevent piracy, a problem which was currently all too common along the coast of China. No incidents developed on the voyage, but the need for such preventive measures seemed evident to those on board.

De La Croix, however, did not demonstrate that the mid-Pacific carried the same degree of risk from piracy as did the China coast, nor did he show how a British ship could both require and then acquire two dozen qualified Chinese seamen, more than half of her crew, in Los Angeles which was simply a bunkering stop.

He also disregarded the storm as a major peril to the *Asiatic Prince,* with force 11 and 12 winds pounding on the ship and building enormous seas for several days. The Rio Cape Line, a Furness Withy subsidiary which operated the *Asiatic Prince*, argued the impossibility of de La Croix's scenario, pointing out that a storm severe enough to put the ship at risk of foundering was an unlikely time and place for launching a mutiny and seizing her. The French writer acknowledged the awkwardness and untimeliness of those circumstances, but insisted, perhaps a bit lamely, that the storm might have coincided with a mutiny possibly provoked by the discovery of the Chinese seamen, who were then obliged to launch their assault a week before the date planned.

In any case, given the wide divergence between the views of these two writers, it becomes difficult to get information and informed opinion on the fate of the ship. Thus, it might be wise to shelve the pirate theory for the moment, and take a look at more conventional explanations of what might have happened to the *Asiatic Prince*, including even some of the possible but unlikely causes such as the meteorites which Villiers railed against.

Like other Prince Line ships, including a group built in German yards, the *Asiatic Prince* was well-constructed. Her Hamburg-built sisterships all survived their peacetime encounters with the sea, although the *Javanese Prince* and the *Chinese Prince* were torpedoed in 1941 and the *Japanese Prince* met a similar fate in 1943, while only the *Malayan Prince* survived the war and was scrapped in 1950.

In trying to account for the disappearance of a seemingly well-built and skillfully-operated ship such as the *Asiatic Prince*, one of the difficulties grows out of a lack of weather reports from ships known to be in stormy seas near the point where missing ships have made their last radio transmissions. None of the three mid-Pacific missing ships in this chapter appear to have vanished in a storm extreme enough to have prompted a general message from another ship in the area describing the location and intensity of the storm.

Such reports would be useful to potential rescuers or investigators, and later historians, in assessing the winds and seas as threats to the missing ship. Radio reports, however, are frequently not forthcoming. To protect the vessel against damage claims, details of weather conditions *are* generally noted in the ship's log. These entries are often exaggerated, suggesting potential harm to vessel or cargo. Perhaps it is an extension of the reluctance of captains to admit, through no fault of their own, that they have come into harm's way. Another possible explanation for this reluctance to share weather information by radio might be that it is regarded as proprietary information, generated on board for use on board. In any case, it is frustrating not to have the assessment of nearby mariners of the meteorological conditions that may be overwhelming a ship.

Lacking information about the intensity of the storm, we can only speculate that the radio antenna carried away, eliminating any chance to call for help, and that something else sank the vessel: the cargo might have shifted, a tsunami or rogue wave may have knocked her on her beam ends, hatch covers somehow came off, a chemical explosion from cargo or some type of explosion may have blown a hole in the hull, or any number of other rare but conceivable accidental causes.

It is difficult to abandon the search for a ship that seems to have conducted herself properly, except perhaps for a heavy-handed radio operator who put an extra dash in her call sign, but nothing more in the way of creative speculation seems possible. Symbolically, after stopping to offer a prayer and to toss a wreath into the water, it is time to move on.

The third of the missing mid-Pacific ships was the *La Crescenta*, a British tanker of sorts which vanished in 1934 in roughly the same area as the *Asiatic Prince* in 1928. Hers was a pathetic case. An eleven-year-old ship she should have been in reasonably good condition, but her niggardly owners cut every corner possible in the maintenance of the ship, and she was in deplorable condition when lost. Alan Villiers was one of the few authors drawn to this ship, apparently in protest over the danger that merchant seamen were forced to endure in sailing such marginal vessels during the worldwide depression of the 1930s. He called her story "a tragedy of the bad days of shipping which, it is to be hoped, will never come again."

La Crescenta was built in 1923 at the Furness Ship Building Company at Haverton Hill on Tyne on the northeast coast of England. Originally laid down as a freighter for a Norwegian firm, she was converted to a tanker while under construction for new owners, Crescent Navigation Company. Crescent was one of those one-ship operations which functioned more as a holding company than a bona fide shipping firm. The day-to-day operations of the ship were in the hands of a managing company, Harris & Dixon.[14]

The vessel was of medium size at 400 feet in length, 53 feet in beam, and 33 feet in depth, and measured out at 5,880 gross tons. She was powered by a triple expansion reciprocating steam engine. Although a modern tanker for that time, everything about her suggested economy. She was apparently conceived to be a tramp tanker, rather than a ship that oil companies or ship brokers would want to charter for extended periods of time.

As a no-frills vessel *La Crescenta* was able to keep reasonably busy during the lean post-war years when too many ships and too few cargoes were available, and on into the depression years when shipping rates plummeted further. She was laid up for a year, during which time it is unlikely that her deferred maintenance jobs were carried out or that she improved operationally. She did manage to stay out of trouble with regulatory authorities, however, and these agencies empowered her owners to add a few extra inches to her load-lines so she could carry additional cargo — provided certain structural components were strengthened. The owners accepted the deeper draft, but neglected the hull strengthening.

Labor costs are a major element of the costs of shipping. Consequently, the company through the years whittled away at the work force on *La Crescenta*. She originally carried a crew of forty, but by 1934 that figure was reduced to twenty-nine. For comparison, a T2 American tanker in World War II would carry a minimum of about thirty-six men.* Today, crews are smaller than those of World War II ships, but in the 1930s the number of crewmen varied between thirty-five and forty per ship.

A "cheap" non-union company in those days could also find ways to get additional work from seamen beyond their traditional duties. The best example was in the deck department, where the captain could relieve the day watches of the mates on the bridge, freeing up those officers to work on deck with the unlicensed crew on routine maintenance projects. While it might seem as if *more* maintenance could be accomplished that way, consider that the company might be getting by without a boatswain, carpenter, and pumpman while using mates to accomplish the work of those men.

Evidence from post-disappearance legal actions against the Crescent Navigation Company in England showed that such procedures were commonly used on its ship, along with a number of other sharp practices and corner cutting designed to save money. The net effect of ten years of this kind of operation was a neglected ship in poor condition. This was the state of the *La Crescenta* as she loaded crude oil at Port San Luis on the central California coast in November of 1934.

A dozen years earlier Port San Luis, previously known as Port Harford, was the leading crude oil loading port in the world, but the growth of the oil industry in the Middle East relegated it to the role of a distant also-ran. Still, it was a logical place for a tramp tanker to acquire a cargo, and the captain of the *La Crescenta*, N. S. Upstill, was happy to have a full load for Osaka, Japan. In fact, he was able to cram in 441 tons beyond her capacity, thus satisfying the owners who always pushed him to overload a bit, thereby maximizing cargo revenue. The fact that the ship's draft was 10-3/4 inches beyond its limit concerned

---

* In the deck department were a master, three mates, a radio officer, a pumpman, a bos'n, a carpenter, six able-bodied seamen, and three ordinary seamen; in the engine department, a chief engineer and three assistant engineers, three firemen, three oilers, and a wiper; and in a stewards department, a steward, three cooks and bakers, three messmen, and a sculleryman.

Captain Upstill, but he knew that being a stickler for regulations was an invitation to unemployment in the tight market for ship captains in 1934. It was a gamble, yes, but no worse than the speed-in-fog gambles that many captains regularly took.

The *La Crescenta* steamed out of Port San Luis on November 24, 1934, en route to Osaka, 5,025 nautical miles across the North Pacific Ocean. A great circle route between these ports would pass about 250 miles south of the Aleutians, and those islands in December have force 11 and 12 weather almost a third of the time. Consequently her captain chose to stay farther south.

On December 5, 1934, the 12th day of the passage, she was in radio contact with several ships. At the time of her last transmission that day the tanker was at 34° 51' North latitude, 163° 24' West longitude, or about 900 nautical miles NNW of Oahu. Inasmuch as the lighthouse at her point of departure, Port San Luis, is at 35° 10' North latitude, it is clear that the ship was not using the great circle route; in fact, she might have been sailing on the 35th parallel of latitude. Using the computations for parallel sailing, the distance traveled was 2,095 nautical miles from Port San Luis to the ship's last known location. Incidentally, the latitude of Osaka, *La Crescenta*'s destination in Japan, is 34° 38' N, so it was convenient to stay on the 35th parallel, even though the Great Circle route was shorter.

Unlike the *Asiatic Prince*, the *La Crescenta*'s contacts with the outside world during her final day did not include a distress message. Early on December 5, 1934, she exchanged identities and positions with the *Athelviscount*, a British molasses tanker, with no indication that anything was amiss. Later on the same day the radio operator on the molasses ship had occasion to radio telegraph the crude oil tanker again, but was unable to reach her. From that moment *La Crescenta* was never seen or heard of again, nor was there any trace of her in the way of wreckage, boats, or bodies.

At the time of her last transmission the amount of fuel consumed since leaving California had lightened the *La Crescenta* somewhat, but she was still six inches deeper in the water than her load lines permitted. That condition would lead to a general sluggishness on the part of the tanker in responding to heavy seas, and possibly reduce her "righting arm"* in returning to an upright position after rolling.

Significantly, there were no Navy ships dispatched in search of the missing ship. Perhaps this was a reflection of the taut depression-era naval budgets, or perhaps no search was launched for the *La Crescenta* simply because she sent no distress message whereas both the *Elkton* and the *Asiatic Prince* did so.

It is not clear when the *La Crescenta* was first posted as missing, but in May of 1935 the Board of Trade conducted a hearing in London into her missing status and that of three other British tramp steamers, all freighters, which also went missing in the Atlantic during the fall and winter — with a total loss of ninety-seven British seaman. Following a preliminary inquiry into the undermanning and lack of seaworthiness of these ships, the Board proceeded with an extraordinary degree of intensity and thoroughness. Taking testimony and evidence from a wide variety of sources, it determined that:

> The *La Crescenta* could be presumed to have gone down in a position not far from her last recorded position as per the testimony from officers of a ship which had encountered a "lake of crude oil" covering several square miles along that route only a month after her last message.
>
> The ship's fore-and-aft catwalk was of insufficient strength to function properly in protecting the power lines, telemotor, steering gear, and bridge to engine-room communication lines that were part of this vital control/communication link.
>
> Records of previous voyages that she shipped heavy seas even in a moderate gale were introduced, as well as evidence that she partially flooded her engine room at least once before. Moreover, *La Crescenta* leaked badly, and needed many rivets replaced.

---

* A term used in analyzing ship stability. It represents a horizontal component in graphic depictions of the static stability of ships; it connects two vertical components, the forces of weight tending to sink the vessel and the forces of buoyancy tending to float the vessel. The relative length of that horizontal component represents the amount of force that tends to return the ship to a level condition after she has been inclined by external forces such as wind or waves.

The crew was numerically too small to handle emergencies that might arise, and the crewmen would have [been] busy fighting such emergencies when the ship went down, making it impossible to abandon ship properly.

She had repeatedly been overloaded throughout 1934, "in constant disregard of the law," and her master knew that management expected him to overload whenever possible.

Some of the most poignant moments of the hearing came when Captain Upstill's letters to his wife were read aloud, describing his unwilling participation in the overloading, and his own physical labor in the tanks of the ship as part of the cleaning force, along with his officers and seamen, in removing sludge and rust.

Although it is not clear why the inquiry panel made this judgement, they opted for a finding that the ship's engine room flooded, causing her to founder before any SOS could be sent or any lifeboats could be launched. Perhaps wing tanks were involved, providing free surface effect which is another dimension in ship stability, whereby liquid cargoes add additional force during the inclining of the vessel by rapidly gravitating to the downhill side of the tank or hold, thus creating a stronger tendency to capsize than a stable dry cargo would produce.

As noted earlier, the preventive maintenance which might have kept the *La Crescenta* from going missing was obviously not performed, but that omission was partially offset *by* the thorough review of the case made after the fact. British maritime investigative panels seemed to be capable of developing sets of questions which could quickly establish what was known and what was not, relevant or not, useful or not, and a host of other questions designed to advance the inquiry. Granted, not all the other missing ships in this book were registered American when they disappeared, and consequently no clear lines of authority existed in many cases. The utter absence of investigations has left American authorities incapable and perhaps even unwilling to explore the perplexing questions raised by these incidents.

In the case of the *La Crescenta,* British maritime unions were able to put into the record the industry's skimpy levels of payments to survivors of lost crewmen, and the tendency of owners to over-insure their old ships with the expectation that a total loss would generate more income than the prevailing freight rates would return them through ongoing operations. These disturbing realities highlighted the plight of seamen the world over. However, American political reformers later missed an opportunity to use the vanished and unexamined ships under our flag, e. g., the northwest colliers, the *Maverick,* USS *Conestoga,* the *Elkton,* and the *Cynthia Olson,* to expose our governmental indifference to the hazards faced by seamen.

Eventually, the owners of *La Crescenta* were required to pay £3,400 toward the cost of the Board of Trade inquiry. The presiding officer appointed by the Board to conduct the inquiry, Lord Merrivale, former president of the Admiralty Court, was highly critical of the way Crescent Navigation Company conducted itself in operating such an unseaworthy ship, thus bringing discredit to the British maritime tradition.

In time the Crescent organization corrected its defects, and grew into a large operation, much of which today functions under other names. The name Crescent survives, however, in some parts of the company, and its house flag still depicts the crescent of a waning moon. Apparently no photograph exists of the troubled tanker whose disappearance brought notoriety to her owners.

The ultimate outcome would have pleased the late Sir Alan Villiers who in his final book expressed hurt at the short range outcome which prevailed for the *La Crescenta* and her crewmen, and hope for the maritime industry in the long range in patching up the wounds of severe cost-cutting in the dark days of the depression of the 1930s.

7

THE *HAI DA*

O ne of the more fascinating of the recurring events of maritime history is the total disappearance of a ship in the midst of other perplexing circumstances. In 1937 one of the most baffling examples of such a disappearance occurred when a radio-equipped steel freighter with an ordinary cargo vanished with all hands, only minutes after heading out from an American port into the open ocean in reasonably good weather. The ship's pre-departure activities were cloaked in mystery, and the riddle only deepened in the days and weeks after she sailed. In fact, the story took so many strange turns in its concluding days that it became almost as difficult to define the nature and scope of the mystery as it was to solve it!

What made the series of events doubly bizarre were wild rumors of Japanese naval intervention, a prelude to the opening days of World War II when such rumors were rampant on the west coast of North America. Some such rumors turned to reality when Japanese submarines sank ships along that coast in 1941. Rumors of such happenings in 1937 had an air of credibility about them.

That year has often been regarded as when World War II actually began, even though the official declaration of war between the Allies and the Axis forces occurred two years later. Two major conflicts were underway in 1937 — the Spanish Civil War, and the Sino-Japanese War. By the end of that year, war bonuses were being paid to American merchant seamen whose ships ventured into Spanish or Chinese waters. In addition, a group of federally-owned ships with merchant crews were ordered to avoid the war zones.

The war in Spain was highlighted by the brutal bombing of the town of Guernica by German planes, while the Japanese intervention in China produced the "Rape of Nanking," a holocaust against the natives of that city. Furthermore, the Japanese sank the American gunboat USS *Panay* on the Yangtze River, a foretaste of the Pearl Harbor attack to come.

So, too, did the disappearance of a freighter in 1937 have a connection. The story has complex roots, and an equally complex

The Hai Da*'s disappearance was characterized by confusing clues and a strong hint of fraud — a common occurance in the intrigue of the period just before World War II.* Jeremy S. Snapp.

As USS Quincy, Hai Da *was operated by the U.S. Navy for several years before becoming a Chinese-owned ship operating under the flag of Great Britain.* U.S. Naval Institute.

conclusion without a final resolution. The *Haida* or *Hai Da* was built for German owners at the Doxford shipyard in Sunderland in the United Kingdom in 1909 as the *Vogesen*. She was a medium-sized ship, measuring out at 3,789 gross tons in a hull whose dimensions were 350 feet in length, 51 feet in breadth, and 22 feet in depth. Her reciprocating coal-fired steam engine produced 2,500 shaft horsepower, driving her single screw at a speed of eleven knots.

She experienced a typical knock-about career for a ship of that era. At the start of World War I she was under German ownership and flag as the *Vogesen*. Upon the entry of the United States into the war in 1917 she was commandeered at the port of Pensacola, Florida.[1] She emerged from that seizure as the USS *Quincy*, and was designated a collier by the Naval Overseas Transportation Service, although her military cargoes on three round-trips to Europe were of a general nature.[1] Her only wartime notoriety occurred when she collided harmlessly with a British warship in convoy in April, 1918.[2]

In September, 1922, after five years of naval service, during which she was designated AK-10, she was sold to private American interests who retained the name *Quincy*. After more than a dozen years in the East Coast coal trade, she was sold in 1936 to the Burgeo Steamship Company which changed her name to *Burgeo Star*, and homeported her in Boston, Massachusetts.

In the spring of 1937 Chinese buyers acquired the ship on the East Coast and re-registered her in Shanghai.[3] Her transfer to the Chinese flag ended twenty years under the Stars and Stripes.

Her new name may have been the anglicized spelling of the two Chinese words *Hai* and *Da,* which mean roughly *arrival by sea* or *reaching the sea.*[4] However, the name was commonly written as *Haida* which, in the Pacific Northwest from which she was soon to disappear, is commonly associated with the Haida Indian tribe in British Columbia. Thus, even the ship's name was enigmatic.

Because she carried the name so briefly at the end of her long career, there was little chance that the *Hai Da* would ever be confused with other ships bearing the name. Those other ships using the single word *Haida* included a venerable U. S. Coast Guard cutter and a Canadian destroyer of World War II, together with several yachts (including one that became USS *Argus,* PY-14) plus a number of vessels that used *Haida* as the first part of a compound name.

The new owners of the *Hai Da,* described as a pair of Shanghai business men named Song and Yih,[5] originally indicated the ship would go to China to be broken up. Thus, there was nothing unusual when she sailed from New York in June, in ballast, en route to the Far East. However, she soon departed from the direct route to the Panama Canal by stopping at Galveston, Texas. Here she loaded a cargo of 5,000 tons of bulk sulphur, reportedly to be used by the Chinese government in making gunpowder.[6] She then sailed early in July for the next stop in her odyssey toward the Orient. That stop, according to her original clearance from New York, would be Vancouver, British Columbia, after which she would sail for Pukow, adjacent to Nanking, the Yangtze River port where the government of China was located. Also listed on the notice of her clearance, although misspelled, was the port of Hsiehchiaten, located between Chinkiang and Nanking, where a large chemical plant was located.[7]

The *Hai Da* cleared the Panama Canal on July 13, and moved into the Pacific. Once there, her movements were reported in the

Guide, the West Coast shipping journal, but the facts in those reports differed in some respects from those reported in the *Maritime Register*, the authoritative New York shipping journal, and dates do not always agree. It appears, however, that she went first to Nanaimo, British Columbia, for coal, where she lay for three weeks awaiting orders before arriving in Seattle in late August of 1937.

Once in Seattle, her owners seemed in no hurry to send her on to China. Quite possibly, they were watching events unfold in the Far East. Although Chiang Kai-Shek had not yet abandoned Nanking as the capital of the country, the Japanese had recently implemented a naval blockade of the Chinese coast. Getting the *Hai Da* to the safety of a Chinese port looked more difficult with each passing day, and the deepwater ports on the lower Yangtze would be particularly hard to reach.

Eventually, during a stay in Seattle of almost two months, the registration of the *Hai Da* was changed to the British flag, her third nationality in six months' time and her fourth overall. However, she received only a temporary British certificate of registry. The flag of that nation was then painted on her bridge as an indication to other ships, particularly Japanese vessels, that she was a neutral in the Sino-Japanese War, a somewhat less-than-honest statement.

This change of nationality seems to have occurred rather easily, and may bear further examination. One authority on international law holds that a ship cannot change her flag during a voyage or while in a port of call, except in the case of a bona fide transfer of ownership.[8] In this case the ownership was apparently transferred from the two Chinese men identified as her owners to George E. Marden of Wheelock, Marden & Company. Marden's shipping and shipbreaking operation was headquartered in Shanghai, but eventually had offices in Hong Kong and New York as well.

Despite her new flag, the non-British character of the *Hai Da* was evident in her crew. Her captain was F. C. Norvick, one of a group of Norwegian captains employed by Marden and a veteran of the Chinese coast;[9] her first officer was K. F. Yank, a Cantonese. The two dozen other crewmen were also Cantonese, all of whom reportedly had been screened for their pro-Nationalist political beliefs, an important criterion in faction-riddled China.

The ship acquired a new radio set while alongside the Bell Street pier in Seattle, a circumstance that could later be used in arguing either that she had excellent communication capability or, alternatively, that she had an untested system with possible defects. In the former case, her subsequent loss would necessarily have to be the result of some instantaneous and catastrophic event which happened so quickly that it could not be reported by radio; in the latter, any scenario would be valid. In either case, the new radio suggested that her owner anticipated the need to keep in close touch with the ship, possibly the sort of contact required of a blockade runner.

Any semblance of secrecy that the ship's captain may have desired was lost through the coverage of the ship's stay in Seattle by curious newspaper reporters. In addition to the new radio equipment, newsmen reported on anticipated actions of the ship, including the fact that the captain intended to sail zig-zag courses at night to avoid Japanese warships. They also wrote of the awareness of the crew that they faced possible death in running the Japanese blockade.

The status of the *Hai Da* was further confused on October 15 when the U. S. Marshal's office in Seattle seized the ship for a $20,000 libel (the statement of the party's claim in admiralty law, and the relief or remedy he desires) filed against her, and did not release her until October 20. The libel was initiated by a former crewman of the ship who had been injured in Norfok, Virginia, in March when the ship belonged to American owners. Eventually it was necessary for the new owner to post a bond before the libel could be removed.[10]

With this rather extensive background established, one can trace the movements of the *Hai Da* through her last known hours as suggested by the bits of available evidence. At 9:25 A.M. on Sunday, October 24, 1937, with a thin layer of coal concealing her sulphur cargo from curious eyes, the ship made an unheralded departure from Seattle. No announcement of her sailing appeared in the *Seattle Times* or any other newspaper. According to the *Guide*, the San Francisco shipping publication, she was bound first for Kahului on the island of Maui, some 2,300 miles away (about a nine-day voyage for an eleven-knot ship such as the *Hai Da*) and for Hong Kong, a port exempt from the Japanese blockade. The outport of Kahului on Maui was probably chosen as a mid-Pacific fueling stop, one that would attract less attention from the Japanese than Honolulu.

A photograph, taken only two days before the ship left Seattle, shows the exterior of the ship clearly from a broad-on-the-bow perspective. Several significant features are visible. The British flag can be seen on her bridge-level deckhouse, announcing to the world her British registration. Second, is a pile of what appears to be coal on her main deck, suggesting concerns that she have enough fuel to cross the Pacific. Third, is an antenna rigged between her two masts, with a lead terminating on her main deck aft of the stack, probably at the radio shack. Finally, she is on an even keel and trim, with a forward draft of about twenty-one feet, indicating no overloading. Her name appears clearly on her bow and on her bridge name-board as the single word *Haida*.[11]

After leaving Elliot Bay in Seattle the freighter began the 125-mile trip to the Pacific, winding through the various passages of Puget Sound until she emerged into the Strait of Juan de Fuca. At Port Townsend her outbound passing was noted at 2:30 P.M. by the reporting station of the Seattle Marine Exchange, but no mention of the ship departing this station was made in the *Seattle Times*. The subsequent dropping of her pilot at Port Angeles was her last official contact. Port Angeles also marked the official demarcation between inland and international waters.

Ahead lay the last remaining contact with the shore, Cape Flattery on Tatoosh Island whose lighthouse marked the entrance to the Strait for inbound ships and the gateway to the oceans of the world for outbound ships. The *Hai Da* apparently reached Cape Flattery late on the evening of October 24, but again newspaper

Cape Flattery's lighthouse on Tatoosh Island may have been witness to the disappearance of several ships, but the persistent fog makes it difficult to see anything from that location. Coast Guard Museum Northwest.

accounts, which often indicated the ships that had arrived or departed Tatoosh Island, failed to note the outbound passage of the ship. She probably set a course to the southwest, representing the initial heading for a great circle passage to Hawaii.

The weather was cloudy but moderate. On the afternoon of the 24th there was a southwesterly wind of fifteen knots, characterized as Force 4, a "moderate breeze," on the Beaufort scale, and a light southwesterly swell. Conditions were much the same twenty-four hours later except the wind had veered to the east and freshened to nineteen knots.[12] The darkness provided a degree of cover, an advantage if the captain expected any potential harm to come from an external source.

The area encompassing the approaches to the Strait of Juan de Fuca has always been dangerous: for inbound ships because the fog makes it difficult for mariners to get bearings at the critical moment when a course change to the east is required to enter the Strait, and for outbound ships because of heavy winds and seas from the southwest which set them to the north toward Vancouver Island. Strong currents, often influenced by tide rips, and heavy swells booming in from the far reaches of the Pacific, add to the peril. The area shares with the Columbia River Bar the soubriquet, "Graveyard of the Pacific," and seasoned mariners fully respect the dangers.

Unlike the Columbia River Bar, the approaches to the Strait of Juan de Fuca are characterized by deep water, including an offshore canyon of 150-fathom depth. This reflects the fact that the entire complex of Puget Sound and the Strait is a fjord, rather than a river mouth. For some reason, the Cape Flattery area, as the point at which ships take their departure from a final land-based navigational position, seems to have been the site of more than a few disappearances of *outbound* ships, particularly during the pre-radio era. The deep and surging water has inhibited the search for wrecks through the years.

A sinister curtain of silence now fell over the *Hai Da*. In spite of her new radio, nothing was heard for more than a month. During that time the war in China took a turn for the worse for Nationalist forces, with Chiang Kai-Shek moving the government out of Nanking and up the Yangtze to Hankow and then on to Chungking.

Then, a mysterious item appeared in the New York *Maritime Register* for December 28, 1937. It reported that an unnamed merchant ship had received radio transmissions from the *Hai Da.*

> Call letters of the British steamship *Hai Da* have been reported heard constantly between November 24 and December 4. The following message was picked up on December 2: "Have you any messages for us?" Vessel was reported to be proceeding at economical speed for Hongkong direct. She is estimated to arrive between December 10 and 16. Master refuses to disclose his position on account of fear of Japanese navy.

Other reported versions of this message indicate that the wording above is probably paraphrased; a version cited by Lloyd's of London two weeks earlier contains the same information in slightly different form, but goes on to report that the cargo owners announced on December 9, 1937, that the *Hai Da* was due the following day in Hong Kong.[13] Thus, the seemingly official reporting of both Lloyd's and the *Maritime Register* was subject to variations in content.

Return radio calls transmitted to the *Hai Da* were not answered, so it was impossible to clear up the confusion about her location and intentions. Unfortunately, neither the name of the ship that received the messages nor her location were cited in the news account which was datelined New York City.

During November of 1937 it was not apparent the *Hai Da* was missing, but at the end of that month a San Francisco business publication stated the ship was unreported and that Coast Guard headquarters in Honolulu had asked ships to keep a sharp lookout for her. On December 16, the *Times* of London said Shanghai steamship interests expressed concern about her. On December 27, in a story datelined Honolulu, the *North China Daily News,* a British newspaper in Shanghai, spoke of rumors circulating in Hawaii that "Japanese warships were possibly responsible for the apparent disappearance of the freighter *Hai Da.*"[14]

In the Pacific Northwest the realization that the ship was missing developed slowly. On December 29 the *Seattle Times* observed that the ship might be overdue, while the *Daily Journal of Commerce* of that city ran the same story on December 31. Both publications noted, however, that the company's agent was expressing no fear for the safety of the ship, even though the *Hai Da* was unreported since leaving Seattle on October 24. According to the agent, the ship carried enough coal to last between fifty-five and sixty days. The fact that no one had seen the ship for sixty-six days was explained as possibly due to an unreported layover of several days "at some port."[15]

In mid-January of 1938 the mystery took another strange turn. Debris from the *Hai Da* was found at two locations on the British Columbia coast. Parts of a ring buoy with *Hai Da, Shanghai,* stenciled on it and an oar also bearing the name of the ship washed ashore at Carmanah Point Lighthouse on Vancouver Island, and on the following day another oar and a piece of a door with part of the British flag painted on it were found near Clo-oose, a few miles farther west.[16] These locations are consistent with the places where known local currents, predominantly from the south with a small component from the west, would be expected to carry debris from a ship in trouble a few miles off Cape Flattery. Some of this debris was encrusted with barnacles, indicating that it was in the water for weeks.

It now appeared likely that the ship never got beyond the approaches to the Strait of Juan de Fuca. In fact, James Gibbs who wrote the definitive history of shipwrecks in that area believed that she probably went down southwest of Cape Flattery, and that view dominates much of the speculation about the ship.[17]

No further information about the ship ever surfaced. Eventually the disappearance of the *Hai Da* became official. On April 20, 1938, Lloyd's posted her as missing and presumed lost, and the symbolic bell used for marking such events was tolled. Unlike the other great disappearance at sea of 1937, that of the Lockheed Electra aircraft carrying Amelia Earhart and Fred Noonan on their round-the-world flight, the disappearance of the *Hai Da* produced no search by ships, planes, or coast watchers. By the time that the reality of her non-arrival was finally accepted by the maritime community, there was nothing constructive to be done.

The speculation about the fate of the ship was influenced by three conflicting clues: her non-arrival in Hong Kong, the radio messages she sent, and the debris from Vancouver Island. At that time and through subsequent years a number of theories about the disappearance of the *Hai Da* have been advanced. These cluster around a half dozen distinct scenarios. The first four of these assume that the ship did sink at Cape Flattery, due to a) weather, b) a natural explosion on board, c) a bomb blast on board, or d) a torpedoing or shelling from an external source. All these possibilities require both that the action was so swift and catastrophic as to allow no time for a radio message to be sent, and that each of the later radio messages was a hoax — with an unknown purpose.

The other possibilities include sinking at some other location from any of the causes listed above, or remaining afloat and eventually reaching the Orient, in which case the debris would have to have been a deliberate attempt to mis-lead potential pursuers. The feasibility of each of these theories can now be reviewed briefly.

If the *Hai Da* was lost at Cape Flattery, the weather theory is the simplest explanation. However, weather conditions were relatively benign at the time of her departure. Two other sulphur-laden radio-equipped ships have similarly vanished in coastal waters of the United States — the *Hewitt* off the Virginia Capes in 1921 and the ex-LST *Southern Districts* off South Carolina in 1954 — but in each case weather was a critical factor. With the *Hai Da*, in spite of the debris, weather does not appear to have caused the disappearance of the ship.

Explosions are a different matter; such an event was entirely possible. One major problem with the bomb/explosion theory is that the noise and sight of an explosion would seemingly be noticeable for some distance in all directions, yet no reports of such an event came in from ships or stations. However, fog could have reduced the visibility at the moment, and the sound may have been lost in one of the "silent zones" reported to exist off Cape Flattery in which ships cannot hear foghorns that are quite close to them. With the wind veering around to the east the sound would have been carried out to sea. Also, underwater explosions have much of their airborne acoustic impact muffled by surrounding seawater. The question remains, however, how do those strange radio messages fit into this theory?

Sulphur is not considered a hazardous cargo, but it is flammable and will support combustion. More important, sulphur dust, like coal or grain dust, is subject to spontaneous combustion or explosion, and this possibility must be considered, even though it appears to be an odd coincidence that such an event would occur just as the ship reached the ocean.

The detonation of a bomb is not mentioned as a possible scenario in any of the accounts of the demise of the *Hai Da*. Yet, bombs against civilian targets have been used as acts of war, and could easily have been employed in this case. A time bomb consisting of 369 sticks of dynamite was placed against the hull of a Japanese passenger liner, the 11,662-ton *Hiye Maru* of the

NYK Line at Seattle in January of 1938. One of the conspirators drowned while trying to attach the bomb, which became waterlogged and failed to explode. The surviving perpetrator acknowledged that they had been paid by unidentified "oriental interests."[18] This statement precipitated a quick response by the Chinese consul in San Francisco that his government knew nothing of the ship. Nevertheless, this kind of act may have been part of the broader arsenal of weapons used by both sides in the Sino-Japanese War.

Torpedoing or shelling by another vessel, presumably Japanese, is perhaps the most popular explanation of what happened to the *Hai Da*. This view corresponded to rumors about Japanese naval activity in the eastern Pacific, and corresponded to perceptions of the Japanese attitude prior to the outbreak of World War II. However, two factors work against this hypothesis. First, while the press was making much of the recent detainment by American officials of Japanese fishing vessels in California waters, there is no indication that *armed* Japanese vessels were in northwestern waters at the time. True, rumors of a Japanese submarine force in the eastern Pacific were circulating widely on the West Coast and in Hawaii, but no one had actually sighted such a vessel. The Japanese were heavily committed in China. It is difficult to imagine they would send a ship to wait out the oft-delayed departure of the *Hai Da* for the Far East. Nor would they do so within sight of the American coast. Furthermore, the later radio messages make no real sense under this scenario, unless they were meant to steer suspicion away from a Japanese attack on a ship that was so close to the coast of Washington as to cause a diplomatic furor if discovered.

The second factor working against the theory of a Japanese attack on the *Hai Da* was the action of the ship's owner, George E. Marden, who at the time was procuring ships for the Japanese. American authorities apparently knew little about him, but it seems apparent he was benefitting from being on both sides of the war between China and Japan. Newspaper accounts make clear that his company was highly profitable. In the fall of 1937 he acquired three laid-up freighters from the U. S. Maritime Commission for a total of $194,500, as part of an acquisition of about a dozen surplus American ships. Nine of these ships were resold to the Japanese.

In addition, at the beginning of 1938 he acquired for his own fleet the *Federal*, a former U. S. Shipping Board freighter, and crewed her with Chinese to take a load of scrap from San Francisco to Japan, only to have the crew desert when they learned where they were headed. Furthermore, the *Marne*, a sistership of the *Federal* that was added to the Marden fleet, was actually placed under Japanese registry. Thus, it could be argued that if the Japanese wanted either to acquire or to destroy the *Hai Da*, all they had to do was to go through Marden. The possibilities suggested by this arrangement are endless, and serve as a commentary on how unwise the American program of ship sales was in 1937.

One of the remaining theories of the demise of the *Hai Da*, that she was sunk by the Japanese but not at Cape Flattery, can be disposed of quickly. The same rationale that appears in the previous paragraph applies here: that if the Japanese wanted the ship they could acquire it anytime through Marden. Also, if the ship were sunk elsewhere, it is highly unlikely that the debris would wash ashore on Vancouver Island, so close to Cape Flattery.

The remaining theory, that of a surviving *Hai Da*, now seems to have considerable merit. The radio messages, which have to be regarded as hoaxes if the sinking theory is accepted, begin to

In 1938 the Marne *was sold to Japan. Here she is shown just after completion in 1919.* U.S. Navy.

fit into the story quite comfortably and logically, with the debris itself now appearing to be deliberately planted. However, there is no evidence that the ship ever reached Hong Kong, and no likelihood that she could have reached her original Yangtze River destination. Consequently, she must have been taken elsewhere. Lists of Marden's ships, appearing in Lloyd's *Register* and in company records, fail to show a 1909-vintage freighter of 3,789 gross tons under any name or registry, so perhaps the *Hai Da* also became a Japanese-owned ship.

Several loose ends still need attention before this analysis can be concluded. First is the question of fuel consumption, specifically, whether she carried enough fuel and water for a trip across the Pacific. At the time she was in radio contact with the unnamed ship, she had been out thirty-nine days and anticipated that it would take eight to fourteen days more to reach Hong Kong. Thus, that crossing would call for at least fifty days of sailing, with no refueling. Although her normal fuel consumption rate is unknown, it was probably about thirty tons a day, comparable to that of Shipping Board vessels of the same size and power. To steam that length of time at that rate would require 1,500 tons of coal at a normal consumption rate, but the ship's rated bunker capacity was only 657 tons. With the extra coal she carried on deck and that used as a cover for the sulphur cargo, she might have had 700 tons on board.

However, with a deadweight capacity of 6,500 tons, 5,000 of which was devoted to cargo, she could carry 1,500 tons of fuel and other commodities. Assuming that 200 tons might be needed for the crew's needs and 200 tons for feedwater, perhaps 1,100 tons of capacity could be available for coal. In fact, one report says that the ship loaded 1,000 tons of coal to her existing supply at Nanaimo, British Columbia. If coal consumption could be brought as low as twenty tons per day by using a significantly slower speed, that rate would permit a fifty-five-day crossing close to the limits of her announced potential range.

Curiously, the slower speed had apparently been tested. The *Hai Da*'s trip west from New York to Seattle was carried out with slow speeds and inordinate delays at each port. The final steaming segment from the Panama Canal to Nanaimo required twenty-five days to cover 4,050 miles. Assuming a normal bunker capacity at that time of 675 tons, that trip consumed fuel at the rate of twenty-seven tons a day at 6.75 knots, which appears in retrospect to have been a practice run for crossing the Pacific without a fuel stop. However, why the ship was not sent from the Canal directly across the Pacific, refueling in Hawaii and arriving in Hong Kong in August, was never explained.

Another loose end, of course, is the report of the radio message. We do not know what was actual text and what was second or third-hand paraphrasing, what ship received it, whether the operator on the receiving ship (whose position we do not know) could estimate the distance that the *Hai Da* was from him, or any of a number of details about the transmission, including who notified Lloyd's and the New York *Maritime Register* of its receipt. Thus, it is impossible to assess properly the legitimacy of the message.

George E. Marden is the ultimate loose end in the story of the *Hai Da*, a man who came into the narrative in the middle as the last owner of the ship and left it at the end under questionable circumstances.[19] After exemplary military service in World War I, Marden began his career in China with Maritime Customs, an agency run by the British, and in that role learned the shipping business as well as the business practices of the Far East. He obviously had no particular affinity for the Chinese government, and was pragmatic in deciding how his ships should be utilized. Although he headquartered in Shanghai, he apparently did not share in the perception of imminent war which the shipping community there felt in the fall of 1941. His fleet was heavily chartered to the Japanese and was largely in Japanese ports or waters at the start of the Pacific war. Subsequently his ships were decimated by American planes and submarines.

Marden was interned by the Japanese in Shanghai, but was repatriated along with a number of British and American civilians on the Italian liner *Conte Verde* which rendezvoused with the

Artist's rendering of the Gripsholm *as a World War II repatriation ship.* Publisher's collection.

famous repatriation ship *Gripsholm* in Lorenço Marques in East Africa. While in England during the war he pursued aviation interests and was associated with the Fairey aircraft organization. After the war he returned to the Far East and reestablished his commercial ventures in Hong Kong, where his son and grandson continued the family tradition of being shipowners.

Whether Marden's pragmatism crossed the line into amorality depends upon what happened to the crew of the *Hai Da*. If those men went down with their ship off Cape Flattery from whatever cause, then Marden is freed from any stigma of placing profits over principles. But if the ship is not there, he must assume responsibility for the safety of the captain and the twenty-seven Chinese crewmen who sailed her.

It is difficult to know what conclusions should be drawn from the *Hai Da* affair. The most likely scenarios for the ship's final moments seem to be an explosion at Cape Flattery or a successful crossing of the Pacific — neither of which was a widely-held explanation of her fate at the time she disappeared. It is tragic that no nation investigated the incident either from the standpoint of marine safety, or from the perspective of naval intelligence.

Today, even if the hull of the ship were found off Cape Flattery we would be only half way toward the resolution of the mystery, but at least we could provide closure to the fate of the crew. Even worse, however, if a thorough inventory of wrecks at that location *failed* to find the elusive ship, we would be as far as ever from knowing where she really went.

8

THE RIDDLE OF THE
CYNTHIA OLSON

The fate of the *Cynthia Olson* has remained one of the great mysteries of World War II. Inasmuch as this ship disappeared between Puget Sound and Hawaii early on December 7, 1941, she has generally been considered the first American ship lost after the start of the war in the Pacific. Yet what were presumed to be her final moments — much of which was documented and even photographed as she lingered on for many hours — remain a mystery as no one saw her sink.

The vessel casualty lists issued at the end of the war treated the *Cynthia Olson* as lost without a trace, but in subsequent years some of the mystery has been explained. In post-war reports the Army treated her as presumably lost in a submarine attack, with the footnote that she reported being trailed by a submarine before her subsequent disappearance. The Coast Guard placed her as number one on their chronological list of merchant ship casualties, but other post-war casualty lists ignored her completely. Some of the oversight was deliberate, on the part of agencies or writers that regarded her as a "military," rather than a merchant, vessel at the time of her demise. She was treated that way in an authentic list compiled by the British Admiralty immediately after the war,[1] and in Robert W. Browning's book published by the Naval Institute in the 1990s about merchant ship casualties during the war.[2]

Still other sources speculated only that she was a victim of a submarine attack. She was among twenty-one ships which "disappeared without a trace" that were described by Cdr. Oliver's article in the Naval Institute *Proceedings* as late as 1961, but he mistakenly placed her en route west from Hawaii rather than to Hawaii.[3]

Frequently mis-identified in histories of the war as a wooden vessel or as a steam schooner,[4] the *Cynthia Olson* was actually a Laker, one of a group of more than 300 small steel freighters built by Great Lakes shipyards for the U. S. Shipping Board in World War I.[5] They were 261 feet in overall length, 43.5 feet in beam, and drew 17-20 feet of water. They measured about 2,100 gross tons, and had a speed of nine or ten knots as powered by a reciprocating steam engine producing 1,250 horsepower driving a single screw. Most were originally coal-fired, but many, including the *Cynthia Olson*, were converted to oil. Belying their name, they became popular as ocean-going tramp steamers, and were widely utilized under the flags of a number of nations on the world's trade routes. Even Japan, the nation responsible for the disappearance of the *Cynthia Olson*, acquired a few.

She was built in 1918 as the *Coquina* by the Manitowoc Shipbuilding Company in the Wisconsin city of the same name. Sold by the Shipping Board in 1926 to Pillsbury & Curtis in San Francisco, she was laid up in 1930 when much of the American merchant fleet was idle. While still laid up she became a part of the fleet of the Los Angeles Steamship Company. During successive reorganizations within the shipping industry she was owned by the California Steamship Company, and then in 1935 by the Matson Line which retained her in laid-up status. Matson

Although the Cynthia Olson *'s encounter with a Japanese submarine was documented and photographed, her sinking was never verified. No trace of her crew and lifeboats was ever found.* U.S. Army Military History Institute.

sold her in 1940 to the Oliver J. Olson Company which renamed her for a granddaughter of the company's owner.

The Olson firm had long been prominent in the shipping of lumber, so their newly acquired ship was modified and given typical West Coast lumber-handling cargo gear with four masts to serve double-rigged hatches. When the charter market became lucrative in 1941, Olson bareboat-chartered the *Cynthia Olson* to the U. S. Army Transport Service. She was commanded by Captain Berthel Carlsen, and carried a crew of thirty-two civilian mariners, a large number of whom were Philippine nationals.

All the officers were American, largely married and from California. An exception was the young third mate, a bachelor from Seattle, who had brought on board a kayak, anticipating a pleasant Hawaiian holiday before returning to the mainland for Christmas. The Army placed two enlisted men aboard as part of the crew, a medical technician and a radio operator, as well as a civilian clerk who represented the Quartermaster Corps.

With her specialized rigging and gear the *Cynthia Olson* was eminently suited to handle the cargo she carried for the Army: lumber to build military housing in Hawaii. As was the standard practice among lumber ships, she carried much of that cargo on deck.

Some people are surprised to learn that the Army operated ships, many of which carried cargo. In reality, during World War II the Army went on to operate a huge fleet of various kinds of ships and watercraft that significantly exceeded the number operated by the Navy. Lakers, as the "bottom of the barrel" of available older ships were particularly numerous in the Army's fleet with at least two dozen such vessels, while the Navy which enjoyed better pickings had fewer than half-a-dozen.

The U. S. Army Transport *Cynthia Olson* sailed from Tacoma, Washington, on December 1, 1941, on her first voyage under charter to the Army. Her destination was Honolulu, about 2,400 miles away — an eleven-day voyage for a nine-knot ship. Initially, the passage was routine, with no hint of any difficulty.

On Sunday, December 7, 1941, the Matson passenger liner *Lurline*, two days out of Honolulu en route to San Francisco, received a radio transmission from the *Olson*, then about 320 miles to the north of the liner's position. Some accounts indicate the ship initially transmitted she was being trailed by a submarine,[6] but the message received by the *Lurline* said only, "SOS. Am under torpedo attack by surfaced submarine." The transmission, described by the liner's operator as "with a very steady hand keying," also provided the ship's position which was given as latitude 33° 42' north and longitude 145° 29' west.[7]

The surprised radio officer on the passenger liner asked for confirmation of the attack. A second message from the freighter corrected the first transmission by reporting that the attack was by the submarine's deck gun rather than by torpedo. At this point the signal from the freighter ceased, and the *Cynthia Olson* was not heard from again.

The captain of the *Lurline*, Charles A. Berndtson, who as senior captain was commodore of the Matson fleet, then directed

Overhead view of Matson's Lurline, *which received the SOS message from the* Cynthia Olson. Publisher's collection.

his operators to contact radio naval stations in California and Hawaii with this information. However, they were unable to raise these stations. Nor could the Coast Guard be reached. Finally, the commercial station KTK of Globe Wireless in San Francisco responded to the *Lurline*'s message. Reportedly, this message was received at 9:30 A.M., Pacific Standard Time, or 7:00 A.M. Hawaii time, but in the light of incomplete and conflicting evidence that time may not have been accurate.

The Globe operator then tried unsuccessfully to telephone the Navy's radio station at the nearby Mare Island Naval Shipyard. Finally, he was able to contact the Office of Naval Communications in the San Francisco Federal Building. A few minutes later the news of the Pearl Harbor attack reached the world, and the fate of the *Cynthia Olson* became a low priority on the Navy's list for December 7th.

The fact that the attack on the *Cynthia Olson* was apparently reported before the attack on Pearl Harbor, has raised questions about the timing of the attack on the ship. Speculation eventually arose about whether the attack on the ship occurred before 7:55 A.M. Hawaiian time which is generally regarded as the time of the Pearl Harbor attack and the opening moment of World War II in the Pacific. Consequently several books and articles on Japanese naval activity at the time of Pearl Harbor, making use of reports from the *Lurline* and shore stations, have challenged the prevailing view that the first shots of the war were fired at Pearl Harbor.

The question of the timing of the attack on the *Cynthia Olson* hinges upon several important facts which have not been properly preserved. One was the time zone in which the *Lurline* was operating at the time she received the message from the freighter; another was the exact time of the message in either local or Greenwich time. Recollections of shipboard and shore radio operators disagree with respect to the receipt of the message, and important records and logbooks containing this crucial information have been destroyed.[8]

Thus, we may never solve the riddle of the time of the attack on the *Cynthia Olson*. The destroyed logs were probably kept in Greenwich Civil Time, so there would have been no question of the time of the radio transmissions from the *Cynthia Olson* and the *Lurline*. Without these logs, all that we can safely say is that there is a distinct, even strong, possibility that the attack on the freighter may have preceded the Pearl Harbor attack.

Furthermore, even if it cannot be established without doubt that the *Cynthia Olson* incident was prior to the Pearl Harbor attack, it was certainly among a very few events that coincided with the start of the war — for example, the depth charge attack on a Japanese midget submarine outside Pearl Harbor at about the same time.

Much of the interest in the time of the *Cynthia Olson* sinking is based on the presumption that if that attack had been carried out before the Pearl Harbor attack there should have been time for the report to reach Hawaii and alert authorities to danger. However, it may be naive to assume that such an alert would have resulted in any action. The depth charge attack on the midget submarine that tried to enter Pearl Harbor was reported an hour-and-a-half ahead of the arrival of the Japanese aircraft, yet that report was still slowly working its way through the channels of Army/Navy communication when the planes arrived.

The only first-hand information about the nature of the attack on the *Cynthia Olson* came from the commander of the attacking Japanese submarine. The *I-26* at that time was one of the newest submarines of the Imperial Navy, in service for less than a month. After the war her commanding officer Cdr. Minoru Yokota reported that he had followed the freighter during the night, and surfaced to confront her in the morning, not sure of whether the scheduled Pearl Harbor attack had yet taken place. At a distance of 3,000 meters he ordered a shot across the bow from the sub's 140-millimeter gun. When the ship broke out her American flag but did not stop, he fired again. This time the ship stopped, and lowered two lifeboats. At the time, the sea was relatively calm.[9]

Originally, Lakers were equipped with four 24-foot steel lifeboats, but many of the ships underwent modifications to the midship deckhouse which left room for only two boats. Contemporary photographs of the *Cynthia Olson* show that she carried two lifeboats. These boats, however, provided ample capacity for a crew of thirty-five officers and men.

After the crew took to the boats and were well away from the ship the submarine fired several more shots. The ship did not sink, so Cdr. Yokota ordered a torpedo fired. The torpedo, an unreliable ten-year-old model provided to the submarine upon commissioning, missed the *Olson,* and the ship remained afloat. The submarine commander, aware that the freighter had sent an SOS message, decided to rethink his options in safety and ordered the *I-26* to submerge.

When the submarine resurfaced Cdr. Yokota found the freighter still afloat, and the crew in the boats apparently heading toward Hawaii. The *Olson* had not yet reached the point where the northeast trade winds blow toward Hawaii, so the men in the boats faced a long difficult journey to the southwest. Since the ship had left port before the outbreak of the war, it was entirely possible that her boats were not equipped with sails or otherwise provided with the proper gear for a long voyage.

The submarine commander quickly saw that no rescue vessels or aircraft were in sight. He then ordered additional shells fired into the listing hull of the vessel, bringing the total number fired, according to Yokota's recollection, to between thirty and forty. At this point one of the crewmen on the submarine with the captain's permission took a photograph of the *Cynthia Olson* showing her afire and sinking deeper into the Pacific swells. Finally, after a total of seven hours on scene the *I-26* departed on the surface, with Yokota hopeful but not sure that the ship would eventually disappear. Thus, the actual sinking of the ship was never confirmed by an eye witness.

The crew of the *Cynthia Olson* remained in the lifeboats. According to Commander Yokota, on the following day another Japanese submarine, *I-19*, passed through the area and found them. A Japanese medical officer looked over the survivors, and directed that they be given food. This suggests that the boats were not well provisioned. After this humanitarian gesture the *I-19* also departed the area,[10] leaving the men to face the wrath of the North Pacific Ocean in open boats in December. However, no corroboration of this incident exists, and the chivalry displayed by the submarine commander was not duplicated in subsequent Japanese confrontations with men in lifeboats.

Cdr. Yokota later rationalized that he expected that American ships and planes would soon comb the area and thus find the survivors. After the war, Yokota converted to Christianity, and apparently the act of leaving the men alone so far from land continued to bother him.[11]

The location given by the *Cynthia Olson* in her distress call was a bit closer to Honolulu to the southwest than to San

Francisco to the east which was about 1,100 miles away. It was a lonely stretch of ocean, well north of the great-circle trackline from California to Hawaii, in an area unlikely to be traversed by many ships or planes. Subsequently, no trace of the men or the lifeboats was ever found.

One prominent historian of the events of Pearl Harbor claims that no mention of the loss of the *Cynthia Olson* appeared in public print until more than a year after the war, but San Francisco papers and the Associated Press reported the ship's disappearance within a few weeks. It is quite possible, however, that no alert to vessels near the area was issued promptly enough to permit the men to be found alive.

Contrary to another assertion by the same historian, the Navy knew of the incident, and has maintained a file of what it knows about it. This file was utilized by a journalist, Alf Pratte, who wrote an accurate five-part account of the *Cynthia Olson* events in the *Honolulu Star-Bulletin* for the 25th Anniversary observance of Pearl Harbor. The file was consulted in the development of this account of the ship's disappearance, as was Pratte's well-written account.

The two submarines that were part of the *Cynthia Olson* story went on to additional stepped-up offensive action. Each fired shells, albeit ineffectively, along the West Coast of North America soon after the start of the war. The *I-26*, which presumably sank the *Cynthia Olson*, then torpedoed the American aircraft carrier USS *Saratoga* in January 1942 southwest of Oahu, putting her out of service for five months. In June she sank the small freighter *Coast Trader* off the Washington coast. In November she torpedoed and sank the cruiser USS *Juneau* with the famous five Sullivan brothers aboard. By the time she sank the merchant ship *Richard Hovey* in 1944 her captain (no longer Cdr. Yokota) demonstrated the prevailing attitude of Japanese submarine commanders toward survivors of torpedo attacks — he ordered the lifeboats of the sinking Liberty ship strafed with machine gun fire and rammed by the submarine.

The *I-19*, which provided food to the men in the lifeboats of the *Cynthia Olson* later sank the carrier USS *Wasp* in September of 1942. Both submarines eventually became victims, with the *I-19* being sunk by surface craft in November of 1943 and the *I-26* by carrier aircraft in November of 1944.

We now move to the more nebulous part of the mystery, the aftermath of abandoning the ship. The *Cynthia Olson*'s many hours afloat following the submarine attack raised the question of what that resiliency foretold for the fate of the ship. Given the condition the ship was in at the time the submarine departed, it is unlikely the crew would have attempted to reboard her. But was she derelict for additional hours or even days? What happened to her deck load of lumber?

Although the *Cynthia Olson* should no longer be regarded as vanishing without a trace, a real mystery still surrounds her final fate. Presumably, she sank, inasmuch as she was fairly deep in the water, on fire, and listing markedly when last seen by her Japanese attackers. Photographic evidence, a rarity in ship disappearance cases, is testimony to her marginal condition at that point.

However, as a relative of the third mate pointed out after the war, no trace of the large deck load of marked lumber was ever found. Prevailing winds and currents probably would have taken the ship, the lifeboats, and any lumber debris toward the North American coast. In fact in recent years the flotsam of ships that have in documented incidents lost containers with such interesting items as rubber-duck bathtub toys and running shoes in them and which have subsequently been found on beaches in the Pacific Northwest, has created much interest in the plotting of these currents by oceanographers.

Then, too, there is the ongoing friendly debate among seafarers in the lumber trade on the question of whether steel ships with lumber cargoes can sink. There seems to be a consensus that wooden ships with lumber cargoes will stay afloat, but the answer with respect to steel ships and lumber cargoes is not as immediately forthcoming. There is no question as to the existence of strong buoyant forces in the lumber cargo tending to keep the ship afloat as opposed to the weight of the steel vessel whose hull has been penetrated and has become a force dragging the vessel down. Can the light displacement tonnage of a Laker, about 2,200 tons, which tends to sink, be offset by 3,500 or 4,000 tons of a lumber cargo which has a tendency to float (but also has weight that adds to the ship's weight)? The answer has apparently never been worked out by scientists in a model basin or a computer simulation.

The mystery of the crew is even greater, and even more frustrating. At one point there was speculation that they might have been picked up by the submarine and taken to Japan as prisoners. Certainly, the Japanese would soon be taking merchant seamen as prisoners; even *I-26* in later incidents picked up a few. However, on December 7, 1941, Japanese submarines were so far from home and their supplies stretched so thin, this scenario seems unlikely. Moreover, Japanese submarine commanders made no such claim.

The Army, however, persisted in the idea that prisoners may have been taken. In 1947, quoting a report originating in the office of the Chief of Transportation, a memorandum to the casualty section of the Adjutant General's Office invoked the Navy as a source in saying:

> ... on January 22, 1942, a dispatch from the Commanding Officer of the 13th Naval District by dispatch to Navy Department, January 22, 1942, stated in substance that in view of having received no reports of any trace of the vessel, appurtenances, cargo, or personnel, and in consideration of the amount of traffic passing in vicinity of the last reported position of the *Olson* and the nature and type of stowage of the cargo carried by the *Olson,* it is very possible that the vessel has been taken as a prize by the enemy.[12]

In spite of this suggestion, the men have never been accounted for. Even worse, no one seems to have tried to determine their fate.

Apparently, no systematic search was ever made, although the memorandum quoted above goes on to refer to a destroyer

HMCS Prince Robert, *a Canadian auxiliary cruiser reversed course and searched the area of the attack for survivors.* airmuseum.ca/rcn/princes.

searching the area. In any case, little if any word was ever passed to ships to keep an eye out for the lifeboats. It is reasonable to assume that during the disorganized days early in World War II only limited searches at best would have been mounted for overdue vessels. Nevertheless, it seems unfair that the *Cynthia Olson,* for whose sinking the time, place, and perpetrator were reported during the very time at which it occurred, could not have been given more attention, then and in later years.

Although no American ship tried to locate the crew of the *Cynthia Olson*, one search effort was undertaken by what amounted to a passer-by. The Canadian auxiliary cruiser HMCS *Prince Robert*, a converted passenger liner from the Canadian Pacific west coast fleet, was en route home from Honolulu to British Columbia and passed through the area where the *Olson* was last seen. In the same message which she received from Canadian authorities alerting her to the Pearl Harbor attack, the cruiser was told of the submarine attack on the *Cynthia Olson*. On his own initiative the captain of the cruiser reversed course at full speed and went back 150 miles to search for the *Olson*. His ship eventually covered an area of 2,400 square miles in an all-night search but found no trace of the freighter or her boats. A Canadian report of this search indicates the night was clear, the sea calm, and the moon "brilliantly full." They found no trace of the ship or her survivors.[13]

This unsuccessful search was made during the night of December 7th. During daylight hours on the 8th the Japanese submarine *I-19* found the two boats in daylight. Since the cruiser would have had the last-known position of the *Olson* as sent in her distress message, she was seemingly in the proper area during her search, but simply did not have the luck to find the American mariners in the dark. Consequently, the final and best opportunity to locate the ship and her crewmen slipped away as the *Prince Robert* resumed her passage to British Columbia.

Curiously, either some sloppy scholarship has crept into the story of the *Cynthia Olson*, or a critical error was made in the reporting of her position. In the original SOS message her location was given as 33° 42' north, 145° 29' west. It was in this location that the *Prince Robert* conducted her search. However, one major source dealing with the loss of the ship cites both the captain and the diving officer of the submarine as reporting their position during the attack as 29° north and 140° west, some 385 miles to the southeast. Apparently no one has compared this major discrepancy in the two reports.

The orderly abandonment of the intact ship by her crew, as witnessed by the Japanese, suggests that the ship's personnel, in terms of skills, were properly distributed between the two boats. Also, there was time enough to take navigational equipment into the lifeboats. This equipment probably included a sextant, chronometer, charts or plotting sheets, and a copy of the current *Nautical Almanac*. If these materials were available in the boats there was no compelling reason why the crew could not have sailed to Hawaii, or at least down into the main steamer track between Hawaii and San Francisco. The sea, however, takes no heed of logic, and the men in the boats may have simply been overwhelmed by the relentless pounding of the ocean as the weather worsened seasonally.

An examination of the experiences of other victims of Japanese submarines in the general area of Hawaii may be helpful in understanding the problems of the survivors of the *Cynthia Olson*. A lifeboat from the Matson ship *Lahaina*, which was shelled and sunk by another Japanese submarine later in December, spent ten days in reaching Hawaii, but the ship was closer when attacked, only about 700 miles north of Maui whereas the *Olson* was at least 930 miles from that island.[14] Also, the Matson crew made use of a sail in covering the distance, and they were in the main steamer lane between Hawaii and the mainland which increased their chances of being found. Inasmuch as all thirty-four crewmen were in the one boat, food and water were in short supply even though the galley refrigerators were raided as the crew prepared to abandon ship. Several crewmen died during the voyage, and others had become crazed after drinking seawater.

At about the same time, the *Mahini*, also of Matson Line, was torpedoed by a Japanese submarine while about two hundred miles south of Hawaii. Although they saw several aircraft pass overhead, the men in the two lifeboats were not found for many days. One boat spent twelve days and the other nine days before being picked up by rescue vessels. Each boat was equipped with sails, but strong counter-currents and winds made it difficult to reach the islands.[15]

Reviewing these experiences of other lifeboat crews in similar situations, it is easy to understand why the men of the *Cynthia Olson* may have been unable to overcome headwinds and other hostile features of their environment. Even if they had sails, and there is no assurance that they did, reaching the nearest of the Hawaiian isles might have taken perhaps twenty days, and for the typical merchant seaman of that era, exposure to the raw winter elements of the North Pacific for that amount of time could easily be too much to handle.

The naval significance of the sinking of the lumber-laden Laker may be that it marked the farthest penetration east by the Japanese task force that attacked Pearl Harbor. Those aboard the *Lurline* can be grateful that Cdr. Yokota waited for his prey along the less-traveled Puget Sound to Hawaii track, rather than the San Francisco-Hawaii route. Furthermore, by taking seven hours in trying to dispose of the *Cynthia Olson* the Japanese commander may also have provided time for the *Lurline* to swing farther south and avoid the submarine.

The *I-26* was built to carry an aircraft, but no plane was in her hangar which was full of fuel to support her cruise to the west coast. For this, too, those aboard the *Lurline* could be grateful, for with a reconnaissance plane in the air the submarine might easily have found the liner and her 784 passengers with disastrous consequences.

Thus, even in her disappearance the *Cynthia Olson* did what Lakers were supposed to do in World War II — buy time for other and more important ships. In staying afloat for at least seven hours, during which time she kept her Japanese attacker occupied, she played her role well, thus justifying far better reviews than she has yet received from historians.[16]

Apparently, the *Cynthia Olson*'s place in history has now been established; she is recognized primarily as the ship that was attacked by the Japanese simultaneously with the attack on Pearl Harbor, perhaps shortly before or shortly after. As such, she has enjoyed notoriety without fame. Such recognition seems misdirected, however, overlooking as it does the human tragedy in the disappearance of the ship and the thirty-five men aboard her.

It is quite possible that the men of the *Cynthia Olson* perished one by one over the next two weeks. The survivors at Pearl Harbor at least learned what happened that day, and who was the enemy in the war that had just begun for the United States. In the lifeboats of the *Cynthia Olson* no such understanding existed, unless someone aboard the second submarine explained the violent events of the previous thirty-six hours. It has not even been confirmed that this encounter took place.

Regardless of whether that briefing happened, it is not difficult to imagine the voices of the crewmen in the boats, diminishing in number and strength as the days passed, asking "Why me, Lord?"

EPILOGUE

Writers of the past have often used a maritime metaphor in concluding their narratives. The comparison is usually to that of a ship captain determining his position after a period of limited visibility in which precise navigation was not possible. Perhaps the greatest example of this occurs in Daniel Webster's famous reply to Senator Robert Hayne in 1830:

> When the mariner has been tossed for many days, in thick weather, and on an unknown sea, he naturally avails himself of the first pause in the storm, the earliest glance at the sun, to take his latitude, and ascertain how far the elements have driven him from his true course. Let us imitate this procedure, and, before we float further in the waves of this debate, refer to the point from which we departed, that we may at least be able to conjecture where we are.[1]

This "whither are we tending" approach has relevance in many settings, including as an appropriate finale for this book. Like a ship's master making a landfall on an unfamiliar coast, we are anxious to know where we are after all the strange turns we have taken. While the reader can best make that judgment, the maritime historian can assist by suggesting where he *hopes* he has taken the reader.

The eight incidents in the previous chapters were each unique, and have led to different conclusions. Briefly, they are as follows:

- The *Montserrat, Keweenaw,* and *Matteawan* were all so new to, and perhaps alien to, West Coast shipping, that they failed to recognize the ongoing dangers in a routine procedure such as taking departure for sea.

- Following her U. S. Navy service, the *Rio Pasig* had an ambiguous identity and nationality which made it difficult for the shipping world to follow her movements, or even to take her seriously.

- The *Maverick*'s several years of tainted obscurity rendered her disappearance unmourned, and her final sightings too bizarre to be taken seriously. The impact of her fate fell unjustly on her crew.

- USS *Conestoga*'s problem in not communicating with the chain of command, and the Navy's bull-headed lack of concern for her, created an unbelievable situation resulting in utter inaction during a desperate crisis.

- The mid-Pacific mysteries of the *Elkton, Asiatic Prince,* and *La Crescenta* highlighted the frailties of both radio communication and rescue capability in that era.

- The efforts of the owner of the *Hai Da* to provide ships to the Japanese, and profits to himself, overshadowed any other theory of her disappearance.

- The *Cynthia Olson* left behind documented last-minute clues, but no empty lifeboats, bodies, or lumber were found to confirm her loss. This "reasonable doubt" may interfere with a clear-cut verdict.

No single over-arcing conclusion can be drawn from these findings, unless perhaps for the six radio-equipped ships. For most of these vessels one can conclude that the lack of radio communication from the ship contributed significantly to her loss. For the *Hai Da* the apparent effort to deceive potential rescuers by means of bogus radio transmissions was unconscionable. Only the *Cynthia Olson* seems to have used her radio wisely during the brief time in which it was in service.

Furthermore, while the question of the odds of any of these ships disappearing has not been explored in any depth, it seems reasonable to conclude that only a slightly different set of voluntary actions might have prevented each loss. However, freeing one ship from that fate might have only shifted the albatross of impending disaster to another vessel.

Even though there has been a certain degree of inevitability present in such disappearances, reflecting such causes as human error, natural causes, or Acts of God, it does seem that counter-balancing forces are at work, and such events might be reduced in the future. The key lies in understanding how such events occur, which is why historians study them.

Fortunately, the types of unexplained disappearances of American ships featured in this book became increasingly rare in the latter decades of the 20th century. In an index of maritime casualties maintained by the United States Coast Guard the last entry which uses the word *disappearance* to characterize the fate of the vessel is that of the SS *Poet* in the Atlantic in 1980. That ship, in spite of sophisticated highly-technological processes used in determining her fate, remains un-traced.

Keep in mind, too, that the declining number of American ships disappearing at sea may be an illusion when one considers our entire merchant fleet has shrunk to a level of only a few hundred ships. Thus, if we were experiencing, say, one such loss a year in a fleet of several thousand ships, that ratio applied to a fleet of several hundred would result in few, if any, disappearances.

Furthermore, in the face of declining numbers of such spectacular disappearances of American ships, it is unwise to conclude that the world has seen the last of such events. Other records of marine casualties, maintained by entities with a more international perspective than that of the U. S. Coast Guard, continue to document ships disappearing under a variety of circumstances. Clearly, despite decades of improvement in shipboard safety equipment, as well as enormous advances in wireless communication systems, ships still vanish from the earth at a disturbing rate.

In the mid 1970s Captain Alan Villiers, whose wisdom we have utilized frequently in this book, in the preface to an updated edition of his book *Posted Missing,* lamented,

> Stress! Stress upon seamen to hurry up, rush faster, turn round with greater speed in ever more enormous, more expensive ship-monsters: stress in the smaller ships too, the fishermen and all the hard-working little fellows that do half the seafaring on earth — this also increases. I suggest that the stress on many seamen today is greater than ever before in man's seafaring history, and in this may lie in part at least the explanation for this odd and continuing phenomenon of the Posted Missing merchant ships.[2]

Two decades later, early in the 1990s, William A. O'Neil, the Secretary-General of the IMO (International Maritime Organization of the United Nations) described the ongoing problem of protecting the safety of passengers and crewmen at sea. He observed that problems still exist, notably that, "The stability of roll-on/roll-off passenger ships continues to give cause for concern, as does the continuing loss of bulk carriers, many of which have vanished without a trace in the past year."[3] It should not be necessary to point out that "many" and "without a trace" are frightening words in a world that prizes its technological solutions to human problems.

While roll-on/roll-off passenger ships, principally in the form of ferries on ocean runs of up to several hundred miles, remain a serious problem for passenger safety because of the problems associated with their bow doors, they generally do not vanish in the sense that term has been used in this book. They may indeed sink with heavy loss of life, but their general location is well enough established to permit rescue and salvage. It is those "many" bulk carriers alluded to by O'Neil, the authentic tramp steamers of this era of seafaring, that are the ships that tend to vanish, and those that lie beyond the reach of rescuers or salvors.

Indeed, bulk carriers continue to be a problem. In connection with the twenty-year investigation of the British *Derbyshire*, one of the websites on that ship reported that "Since 1980, over 240 bulkers (greater than 10,000 DWT [Dead Weight Tons]) and approximately 1,500 mariners have been lost. At least twenty-two of these bulkers have disappeared without a trace."[4]

The sea continues to be a perilous workplace. At about the same time that Secretary-General O'Neil made his statement about ongoing safety problems, a new journal in the American maritime industry was launched. This magazine, *The Professional Mariner*, is directed toward those men and women who make their living as seafarers. The first issue, as well as every regular issue since, contains a feature section on "Maritime Casualties." It has become a popular section among readers, many of whom may have a "there, but for the grace of God, go I" reaction as they read the accounts of maritime accidents. The volume of material appearing in that section is heavy enough to justify a full-time editor.

While most of that material is concerned with small scale accidents, albeit often with fatalities, there are occasionally accounts of serious tragedies at sea that involve a foundering and less frequently the disappearance of a ship. There have also been accounts of derelicts which continue to elude detection and "capture." Thus, Joseph Conrad's notion of the sea as a never changing force of nature, which he espoused in *Typhoon* in 1902, remains valid more than a century later.

However, one less-than-subtle change may have occurred. The most widely-suspected reason for the disappearance of ships seems to have shifted from the natural phenomena and human errors of the past to a new scourge, or rather an old scourge with new high-tech weaponry, that of piracy.

Modern piracy runs the gamut of activities from simply boarding vessels and robbing crewmen or passengers, to taking a ship, killing the crew, and changing the ship's identity and nationality, after which she is often put back into service in legitimate trade. This is possible because of the loose regulatory environment in much of the third-world, as well as the physical sanctuary available in the many remote hiding places along the lengthy coasts of such nations as Indonesia, and more recently Somalia.

An extensive daily log of such acts of piracy, as well as other maritime casualties, is displayed on an internet website called "Cargo Law," maintained by an admiralty law firm in Los Angeles.[5] That source is a revealing and frightening reminder of how lawless the sea can and has become.

Monetary gain has been the principal motive for pirates, but today there is potentially an even more insidious motive, ideology. Religious fanatics, acting as terrorists rather than as traditional pirates, could easily include killing a ship's crew and the commandeering their vessels into a repertoire of evil as a dual means of proclaiming the faith as well as raising money to support their other operations. We can only hope this grim scenario does not flourish.

Fortunately, the loss of ships from more traditional causes is being countered by a new science known as marine forensics. Utilizing deepsea exploration and the experimental facilities of model basins and materials labs, scientists are able to find ships once considered lost, and offer explanations of their fate.

Obviously, such an approach is effective only within and among cooperating nations with a system of criminal justice that assigns and enforces responsibility.

One of the most startling demonstrations of this marine forensic capability came in the year 2000 in the case of the *Derbyshire*, a British bulk carrier which had vanished in the Far East during a typhoon twenty years earlier. Photos taken of the hull, discovered in 1994 in 13,500 feet of water, showed strong evidence of a structural hatch-cover failure, and subsequent tests in model basins bore out this theory of her loss. These discoveries relieved the ship's long-dead crew of culpability or neglect in carrying out their duties, thus rewarding the organized and extended efforts of surviving family members of the crew of the ship.

There is also serious discussion of using a black box, similar to that found on airplanes, to solve the riddles of maritime casualties. Not only do we need such a record of ship movement and performance, we also need better measures of identity. In the past the only permanent indication of the identity of a ship was her official number, burned into her main structural beam or a hatch coaming. Today, the pirate who can forge new registration papers for the ship as readily as he can repaint the ship's name on her stern can probably also alter that official number with modern technology at his disposal.

However, the issue of the right of privacy, may have a natural parallel, extending from people to the tools or artifacts of people, specifically ships. If every ship were required to have an electronic signature monitored by satellites, ships losses to all causes, including piracy, could be reduced significantly. But the same questions asked with respect to fingerprinting or DNA-coding of every citizen of a democratic nation in the name of crime prevention can be asked about such an Orwellian measure to prevent the loss of ships: is this the kind of world we want?

Given the extremes of unscrupulous rulers and impotent nations in the world, it may be difficult to find a quick solution to the piracy problem. Consequently, it would be easy to long for the good old days when ships vanished with some regularity but only from natural causes or human error, with an occasional piracy thrown in to keep mariners from getting too complacent. We have come too far, however, in the technology and methodology of ship management to want to return to those days, a time when hundreds of lives could be lost annually to ship disappearances. Using all our newly acquired resources, it is important to work toward the elimination of ship disappearances — including those resulting from piracy — because such events result in the loss of valuable human lives and costly resources, as well as rendering the oceans of the world a lawless frontier.

At the same time, we can continue to look back on the centuries of ship disappearances with the same sense of respect and even admiration that we accord to those who have fallen in battle. Just as honoring war dead is not an endorsement of war, learning about and honoring those who have perished on vanished ships is not an endorsement of the causes of such disappearances.

Meanwhile, ships will continue to disappear. During the writing of an early draft of this epilogue an incident occurred in the Indian Ocean, illustrative of one cause of such disappearances: the ravages of time exacerbated by inadequate vessel maintenance. A thirty-year-old tug, originally designed as an anchor-handling tug for oil rigs, became separated from her tow which was an overmatch for her — a 16,000-ton bulker en route to scrapping in India — and vanished without a trace, with a dozen crewmen aboard. The tug was as much a candidate for scrapping as was her tow. She was acquired in Trinidad in a fire-damaged condition, and mid-way through her initial voyage for the new owners she put into Walvis Bay in Numibia on Africa's southwest coast for extensive repairs.

When the derelict ship was later located, the remnants of jury-rigged towing gear on her showed that the tug had made several efforts to recapture her tow, but failed. What ultimately happened to the 130-foot tug is anyone's guess.[6]

This recent and sobering reminder of the risk of ship disappearances marks an appropriate point at which to end this narrative. A fitting final reflection might be, there is nothing romantic about a ship sailing off into oblivion; there is only the abhorrent ugliness of many deaths that might well have been prevented. While there may be a fascination for mankind in such mysteries, we need not feel guilty in having such feelings of curiosity as long as we temper them with concern for the tragedy these events have forced upon the innocent victims and their families.

END NOTES

Chapter 1

1. Edward F. Oliver, "Overdue - Presumed Lost," *Naval Institute Proceedings*, March 1961, 98-105.

2. For a brief account of this vessel see *Dictionary of American Naval Fighting Ships* (Washington, DC: Naval Historical Center, 1959-81) hereafter cited as DANFS, v. 2.

3. James A. Gibbs, *Disaster Log of Ships* (New York: Bonanza Books, 1971), 160.

4. Quentin Reynolds, *Officially Dead: The Story of Commander C.D. Smith* (New York: Random House, 1945), 92-95.

5. Reynolds, 97-99.

6. *San Francisco Chronicle*, December 13, 1917, 2; *San Francisco Examiner*, December 18, 1917, 13.

7. For this and other missing ships of this company see Arthur Gordon, *The Years of Peril* (New York: Socony Vacuum Oil Co., 1994).

8. James A. Gibbs, *Peril at Sea* (West Chester, PA: Schiffer Publishing LTD., 1986) 203.

9. Joseph Conrad, *Lord Jim* (Boston: The Riverside Press Cambridge, 1958).

10. David H. Grover, *The Unforgiving Coast: Maritime Disasters of the Pacific Northwest* (Corvallis, OR: Oregon State University Press, 2002), 156-70.

11. Alf Pratte, "*Cynthia Olson*'s Fate Sealed - but When?," *Honolulu Star-Bulletin*, December 7, 1966, B-2.

12. The basic facts of this case are in Suduffco. 1929 *American Maritime Cases,* 773.

13. Adolph A. Hoehling, *Lost at Sea* (Harrisburg, PA: Stackpole Books, 1999), 130-47.

14. H. L. Holman, *A Handy Book for Shipowners & Masters* (London: Commercial Printing & Stationery Company, n. d.), 223.

15. James A. Gibbs, *Pacific Graveyard* (Portland, OR: Binford & Mort, 1993), 120; author's personal recollections.

16. Walter Jackson, *The Doghole Schooners* (Mendocino, CA: Bear & Stebbins, 1977), 44.

17. Jackson, 32.

18. Cited in Elkton *1929 American Maritime Cases* 1350.

19. David H. Grover, *Captives of Shanghai: The Story of the President Harrison* (Napa, CA: Western Maritime Press, 1989), 130.

Chapter 2

1. E. W. Wright, ed., *Lewis & Dryden's Marine History of the Pacific Northwest* (Portland, OR: Lewis & Dryden Printing Co., 1896).

2. *San Francisco Chronicle,* December 16, 1894.

3. *Lewis & Dryden,* 417.

4. *San Francisco Chronicle,* December 16, 1894, n. p.

5. Captain Davis' assessment of Captain Blackburn and the *Montserrat* is contained in his diary of June 9, 1892, displayed as of March 2010 on the website Micronesia: Marakei at www.janeresture.com/marakei/index.htm.

6. A useful account of the "blackbirding" carried out by the *Montserrat* appears in Arthur Inkersley and W. H. Brommage, "Experiences of a 'Blackbirder' among the Gilbert Islanders," *Overland Monthly,* V. 23, No. 138, June 1894, 565-575. Brommage was aboard the *Montserrat* during her time in the Gilberts, but it is not clear if he made the pending voyage to Guatemala. Another worthwhile account is David McCreery and

Doug Munro, "The Cargo of the *Montserrat*: Gilbertese Labor in Guatemalan Coffee, 1890-1908," *The Americas*, v. 49, No. 3, January 1993, 271-295.

7. *Lewis & Dryden*, 378.

8. *San Francisco Chronicle*, December 19, 1894, n. p.

9. A good summary of this case appears in McMullin *et al* v. Blackburn at *Federal Reporter* 59F1 177.

10. This process is described in Francis G. Jenkins, "The Saginaw Steel Steamship Company and Its Steamers*,"American Neptune*, v. 42, 1982, 245-275. Jenkins' grandfather was master of the *Keweenaw*; his father was second mate.

11. Jack Sweetman*, American Naval History: An Illustrated Chronology* (Annapolis: Naval Institute Press, 1984), 100.

12. "Shields's Brutal Treatment; A Sailor Whom the Chilean Policemen Terribly Abused," *New York Times*, January 12, 1892 n. p.

13. Benjamin Harrison, "Message to Congress Reporting on Correspondence Between the United States and Chile Regarding Violence Against American Sailors in Valparaiso," January 25, 1882. The American Presidency Project, www.presidency.ucsb. edu/ws/index as of March 2010.

14. *Lewis & Dryden*, 417.

15. *San Francisco Chronicle*, 17 December 1894, n. p.

16. Details of the *Matteawan*'s brief career appear in Jenkins.

17. *Red Duster* website, Prince Line, 9. www.red-duster.co/ uk/Prince 9, as of 01-01-10.

18. Charles Dana Gibson, *Over Seas, U. S. Army Operations 1898 Through the Fall of the Philippines* (Camden, ME: Ensign Press, 2002), 20, 38.

19. Burr McIntosh, "The Transport *Yucatan* Nearly Rams the *Matteawan*!," The Spanish-American War Centennial website, www.spanamwar.com/Yucatan, as of 01-01,10.

20. *Red Duster* website, 9.

21. *Red Duster* website, 9.

22. *Lloyds' Register*, 1900, 723.

23. Jenkins, 246.

24. Gordon Newell, editor, *H. W. McCurdy Marine History of the Pacific Northwest* (Seattle. WA: Superior Publishing Co., 1966), 96.

25. Jenkins, 274.

26. Grover, *Unforgiving Coast,* 63-67.

27. James A. Gibbs, *Shipwrecks of the Pacific Coast* (Portland, Oregon: Binford & Mort, 1957), 35-41.

28. Gibbs, *Shipwrecks*, 41.

29. *Lewis & Dryden*, 417.

30. Grover, *Unforgiving Coast*, 69-70.

Chapter 3

1. *Lloyds' Register*, 1916-17.

2. *Japan Times*, May 9, 1916, 8. See also ltr, French Ambassador Jusserand to American Secretary of State Bryan, September 21, 1914 in State Department Decimal File 763.72111/204 in RG 59, National Archives.

3. A useful discussion of contraband and the various rules of neutrality appears in J. W. Hall, *The Law of Naval Warfare* (London: Chapman & Hall, Ltd., 1921).

4. *The Times Documentary History of the War*, Volume III, *Naval-Part 1* (London: Printing House Square, 1917), 376-82.

5. The British list is contained in *British Merchant Shipping (Losses), World War I* (Wellington, NZ: New Zealand Ship and Marine Society, 1966), 1; the American list appears on the authoritative merchant marine website: www.usmm.org., as of March 2010.

6. *Japan Times*, 9 May 1916, 8.

7. *Lloyds' Register*, 1916-17.

8. Movement card for the *Rio Pasig*, San Francisco Marine Exchange, at National Maritime Museum, San Francisco.

9. The *Guide*, San Francisco, 2 January 1916.

10. Details of Waterhouse's career appear in his obituaries in Seattle papers, circa March 21, 1930.

11. The *Times* of London, April 4, 1916, 4.

12. *Seattle Post-Intelligencer*, January 23, 1917, 12.

13. Movement card, *Rio Pasig*, San Francisco Marine Exchange.

14. *Seattle Times*, 12 April 1917, 13.

15. Rumors about submarine parts are described in David H. Grover, *The San Francisco Shipping Conspiracies of World War One* (Napa, CA: Western Maritime Press,1995), 107. A newspaper story about a "knock-down" submarine aboard the ship appeared in the Richmond (CA) *Record-Herald*, November 4, 1915, 1.

16. Pilot Chart of the North Pacific, November, 1953.

17. *Japan Times*, May 9, 1916, 8.

18. Shipping columns, *Seattle Times* and *Seattle Post-Intelligencer*, April 9, 1916.

19. Henry Landau, *The Enemy Within* (New York: Putnam, 1937) 25-28.

Chapter 4

1. Grover, *Conspiracies*, 13-24. This source contains much additional information about the *Maverick* and other ships and men of the German-Hindu Conspiracy to send arms to India. Records of court cases growing out of the conspiracies are contained in RG 116 and 118, National Archives, San Bruno, CA.

2. Chief Officer's Log of the SS *Sacramento*, in possession of the author, for November 8, 1914 through November 17, 1914.

3. Much of the information on this stage of the shipping conspiracies is from Ltr, U. S. Attorney John W. Preston to F. H. Duehay, President, United States Parole Board, January 25, 1919, in RG 118.

4. The German-American conspiracies are described in considerable detail in Preston, ltr to F H. Duehay.

5. Memorandum for "Warren," undated and initialed CMS March 21, 1916, in Record Group 116.

6. The movements of the *Annie Larsen* are reconstructed from information provided by crew member Peter Olsen in interviews with federal investigators in November 1917.

7. The initial circumstances and the trip across the Pacific by the *Maverick* are reconstructed from the statement given to Singapore police by John B. Starr-Hunt, supercargo of the ship, May 8-16, 1916 in RG 118.

8. Diary of Cdr. Raymond D. Hasbrouck, USN, former commanding officer of USS *Yorktown* for April 26-27, 1915, abstracted in report of federal agent C. B. Treadway, September 24, 1917, in RG 118.

9. Ltr., W. D. Prideaux, Master, USS *Nanshan*, to Commander-in-Chief, Pacific Fleet, May 13, 1915, in RG 118.

10. Starr-Hunt, statement to Singapore police.

11. Statement of Harry J. Potoff, San Pedro, December 21, 1917, in RG 118.

12. Richmond, CA, *Record-Herald*, November 4, 1915, 1.

13. Ltr, Harry J. Hart to Captain William Kessel, September 20, 1916, in RG 118.

14. Ltr., Captain George MacGoldrick to Collector of Customs, Manila, August 9, 1917, in RG 118. Federal financial support for the transaction is mentioned in *San Francisco Chronicle*, December 13, 1917, 13.

15. Ltr., MacGoldrick.

16. *New York Times*, October 4, 1917, 4, 24.

17. The *Paloona's* encounter with what she thought to be the *Maverick* is described in both the *San Francisco Chronicle*, 2, and *San Francisco Examiner*, 13, for December 13, 1917.

18. *San Francisco Chronicle*, December 13, 1917, 2.

Chapter 5

1. The basic source of information on the loss of the *Conestoga* is RG 45, Naval Records Collection of the Office

of Naval Records and Library, Navy Subject File, 1911-1927, File OS (Ships, U. S. Navy, Commissioned), Box 1070, cited hereafter as File OS. The Deck Log of the *Conestoga* was also consulted.

2. Deck Log of the *Conestoga*, 1917-18.

3. Ltr., CinCPac to OpNav May 19, 1921.

4. Ltr., LCDR E. D. Capehart, USN, July 22, 1921, to M. J. Donovan, states that the telegram concerning the loss of the barge was "incorrect." A similar letter to Elliott W. Sproul, member of the House of Representatives in behalf of a constituent, signed by Theodore Roosevelt, Jr., Acting Secretary of the Navy, was somewhat more conciliatory, saying, "I fail to understand the following statement [relative to the loss of the barge]."

5. Deck Log of the *Conestoga*, 1921-22.

6. W. Somerset Maugham, *"Rain," The Complete Short Stories of W. Somerset Maugham, I, East and West* (Garden City, NY: Doubleday & Company, 1953) 1-39.

7. *San Francisco Examiner*, May 22, 1921, 20.

8. Radio Message, Com12 to OpNav, April 5, 1921, in File OS, Folder 9; Radio Message, CinCPac to OpNav, April 6, 1921, in File OS, Folder 9.

9. The basic details of this adventure appear in the DANFS listing for the R-14.

10. An illustrated account of the *Senator*'s discovery of the lifeboat appears in *San Francisco Examiner*, May 21, 1921, 15.

11. The search armada and procedures are described in the *San Diego Union*, May 21, 1921, 6.

12. Com11 to OpNav, May 8, 1921, in File OS, Folder 9.

13. Radio Message, CinCPac to OpNav, June 10, 1921, in File OS, Folder 9.

14. Statement, Office of Naval Records and Library, Historical Section, June 30, 1921, in File OS, Folder 9.

Chapter 6

1. Captain Edward C. March, "Skinner and Eddy and Their 1105s," *Steamboat Bill*, Winter 1994, 273.

2. Captain Columbus D. Smith in Reynolds, *Officially Dead*, 97.

3. New York *Maritime Register*, February 16, 1927.

4. *Monthly Weather Review*, U. S. Weather Bureau, February 1927, 100.

5. Smith in Reynolds, 98; cited hereafter as Smith/Reynolds.

6. Smith/Reynolds, 98-99.

7. Smith/Reynolds, 99.

8. *Coast Seamen's Journal*, November 1927, 348.

9. E. Kay Gibson, *Brutality on Trial: "Hellfire" Pedersen, "Fighting" Hansen, and the Seamen's Act of 1915* (Gainesville, FL: University Press of Florida, 2006), 133.

10. 1929 *American Maritime Cases,* 1347.

11. Accounts of this incident appear in Smith/Reynolds, 92-95.

12. Most of what we know about the loss of the *Asiatic Prince* comes from the prolific pen of Sir Alan Villiers who in *Posted Missing, The Story of Ships Lost without Trace in Recent Years* (New York, Charles Scribner's Sons, 1974), 278-80, tells the story of that ship as a "genuine sea mystery, a really clueless case."

13. Robert De La Croix, Translated from the French by James Cleugh, *Mysteries of the Pacific* (New York: The John Day Company, 1957), 197-212. His summary of her fate differed from that of Villiers: "The spirit of legend that haunted the Pacific had taken possession of the vessel and carried her off to voyage on the uncharted seas of the imagination of mankind."

14. Villiers, 238-46, singles out this ship as an example of criminal neglect by her owners.

Chapter 7

1. *Dictionary of American Naval Fighting Ships*, v. 5, 415-16.

2. Lewis P. Clephane, *History of the Naval Overseas Transportation Service in World War I* (Washington, D.C.: Naval History Division, 1969), 255.

3. James A. Gibbs, *Shipwrecks Off Juan de Fuca* (Portland, OR: Binford & Morts, 1968), 187.

4. Translation by Dr. John Bow, formerly head of Mandarin at the Defense Language Institute, Monterey, CA.

5. Lloyd M. Stadum, "The *Haida* Mystery," *Sea Chest*, March 1958, 33, gives the name of the two owners as V. K. Song and Z. F. Hwah. The *Times* of London, December 16, 1937, identifies the owners as Song and Yih. H. W. Dick and S. A. Kentwell, *Beancakers to Boxboats: Steamship Companies in Chinese Waters* (Canberra: Nautical Association of Australia, 1988), 169 ff., speak of Yi Zen Fong as the owner of the seven U. S. Shipping Board vessels which had been obtained from the Maritime Commission, so there is some confusion about the first set of Chinese owners.

6. Stadum, 34.

7. This port remained a mystery until James Mossman, an indefatigable researcher at the Puget Sound Maritime Historical Society, found the name on a *Sailing Directions for the Yangtze*. The author is indebted to the late Mr. Mossman for extensive research assistance over the last decade.

8. Burdick H. Brittin, *International Law for Seagoing Officers* (Annapolis: Naval Institute Press, 1968), 132.

9. McCurdy, 467.

10. *Daily Journal of Commerce*, October 21, 1937, 2.

11. This important photograph was taken by John F. Snapp, and appears on p. 88 of Jeremy S. Snapp, *Northwest Legacy: Sail, Steam & Motorships* (Lopez Island, WA: Pacific Northwest Heritage Press, 1999.) It was made available to the author by courtesy of the younger Mr. Snapp.

12. Seattle *Times*, October 25-26, 1937, shipping pages.

13. *Times* of London, December 16, 1937, 22.

14. *North China Daily News*, December 29, 1937, 5.

15. *Daily Journal of Commerce*, December 31, 1937, 2.

16. *Seattle Times*, January 14, 1938, 11; January 18, 1938, 7.

17. James Gibbs, ltr. to the author, November 1, 2003. Gibbs recalled as a boy watching the *Hai Da's* preparations for sea from Queen Anne Hill in Seattle. He leaned toward the explosion theory of her demise.

18. *New York Times*, January 21, 1938, 10; January 22, 1938, 3; January 23, 1938, 34.

19. Marden's career is explored in Dick and Kentwell. Additional information about the man, reflecting personal contact between his daughter and grandson in Hong Kong and the author, appears in the author's "*Haida* Revisited," *Sea Chest*, June 2005.

Chapter 8

1. *British and Foreign Merchant Vessels Lost or Damaged by Enemy Action During Second World War* (London: Naval Staff [Trade Division], Admiralty, 1945).

2. Robert M. Browning, Jr., *U. S. Merchant Vessel Casualties of World War II* (Annapolis: Naval Institute Press, 1996).

3. Oliver, 98-107.

4. Two authoritative Pearl Harbor historians identify her as a wooden ship: Gordon W. Prange with Donald Goldstein and Katherine V. Dillon, *December 7, 1941: The Day the Japanese Attacked Pearl Harbor* (New York: Mc-Graw-Hill Book Co., 1988), and Stanly Weintraub, *Long Day's Journey Into War* (New York: Truman Talley Books, Dutton, 1991). Arthur R. Moore, *A Careless Word . . . A Needless Sinking* (Kings Point, NY: American Merchant Marine Museum, 1983) calls her a steam schooner.

5. The seminal book on steam schooners, Jack McNairn and Jerry MacMullen, *Ships of the Redwood Coast* (Stanford, CA: Stanford University Press, 1945), 108, refers to steel three-island lumber-carrying vessels as "'Lake' steam schooners."

6. Attribution for this report is difficult to re-locate. The author, in his 1987 book, *U. S. Army Ships and Watercraft of*

World War Two, (Annapolis: Naval Institute Press, 1987) repeated, 6, the claim about the ship reporting being trailed by the submarine, but, in an effort to avoid excessive endnotes, failed to cite the source of that information.

7. A useful source of information about the attack is Burl Burlingame, *Advance Force Pearl Harbor* (Kailua, HI: Pacific Monograph, 1992). The reference to the steady hand at the radio key is William L. Worden, *Cargoes: Matson's First Century in the Pacific* (Honolulu: University Press of Hawaii, 1981, 86. The voyage of the *Lurline* is described by her chief officer Edward Collins, "Rendezvous with Destiny: The S. S. *Lurline*'s Pearl Harbor Voyage," *Amp&rsand*, Winter 1991, 4-9. *Amp&rsand* is the house organ of Alexander & Baldwin which has owned Matson for a number of years.

8. The best account of the *Cynthia Olson's* crisis, including the question of the time involved, is in Alf Pratte, *Cynthia Olson's* Fate Sealed — but When?," *Honolulu Star-Bulletin*, December 7, 1966, B-2. Pratte's series of articles over a five-day period in December 1966 commemorated the 25th Anniversary of the attack on Pearl Harbor.

9. Yokota's story is told by Prange, 49, who interviewed him in 1951, and by Bert Webber, *Silent Siege III* (Medford, OR: Webb Research Group, 1992), 22. Webber had corresponded with Yokota.

10. Ltr., Yokota to Webber, September 1983, quoted in Webber.

11. Yokota interview with Prange.

12. Quoted in ltr., March 11, 1947, to Chief, Casualty Section, Personnel Actions Branch, Adjutant General's Office, from Myrta Ethel Cawood, Investigator, Status Review and Determination Sub-Section.

13. M. K. MacLeod, preparer. Canadian Forces Headquarters Report, *The Prince Ships, 1940-1945* (Ottawa: Directorate of History and Heritage, October 31, 1965), 56-57.

14. Hans O. Matthiesen and Douglas McMurty, "Abandon Ship! The S. S. *Lahaina's* Ordeal at Sea," *Amp&rsand*, Winter

1991, 18-21.

15. George W. Jahn, "Survival by Lifeboat," *Amp&rsand*, Winter 1991, 12-17.

16. The ultimate word on the *Cynthia Olson* has now been penned. During the reading of the galley proofs on this book the author was sent a new book on the disappearance of this ship, and the various efforts which have been mounted to learn more about her fate. Readers interested in knowing more about this first American merchant ship to be lost concurrent with the Pearl Harbor attack may wish to read: Stephen Harding, *Voyage to Oblivion, A Sunken Ship, A Vanished Crew and the Final Mystery of Pearl Harbor* (Stroud, Gloucestershire, UK: Amberly Publishing, 2010).

Epilogue

1. William Jennings Bryan, editor, *The World's Famous Orations* (New York: Funk and Wagnalls Company, 1906), 38.

2. Villiers, xxiv.

3. Quoted in extension of remarks, Hon. Walter B. Jones in the House of Representatives, October 21, 1991 (World Maritime Day), appearing on the website of the Congressional Record as of September 15, 2005.

4. Website www.hsreemsnyder.com/derbyshire, as of October 1, 2005.

5. Website www.cargolaw.com. as of October 1, 2005.

6. Website www.abovetopsecret.com/forum as of October 1, 2005. The primary source for the information on this website was the newspaper *Cape Argus* of Cape Town.

ABOUT THE AUTHOR

BIBLIOGRAPHY

INDEX

ABOUT THE AUTHOR

David H. Grover served as a naval and merchant marine officer in World War II before coming ashore to work in broadcasting and as a university teacher and administrator. His last academic assignment was as Dean of the California Maritime Academy. He is a retired commander in the Naval reserve and chief mate in the merchant marine. He has written several books on naval and maritime history focused on the Pacific basin and has served as editor/historian for the Yangtze River Patrol Association. He currently lives in Napa, California.

Bibliography

Books

Action During Second World War. London: Naval Staff [Trade Division], Admiralty, 1945.

American Maritime Cases, 1929. Baltimore: The Maritime Law Association of the United States, 1929.

British Merchant Shipping (Losses), World War I. Wellington: New Zealand Ship and Marine Society, 1966.

British and Foreign Merchant Vessels Lost or Damaged by Enemy.

Brittin, Burdick H., *International Law for Seagoing Officers.* Annapois, Maryland: Naval Institute Press, 1968.

Browning, Robert M., Jr., *U. S. Merchant Vessel Casualties of World War II.* Annapolis: Naval Institute Press, 1969.

Bryan, William Jennings, ed., *The World's Famous Orations.* New York: Funk and Wagnalls Company, 1906.

Burlingame, Burl, *Advance Force Pearl Harbor.* Kailua, HI: Pacific Monograph, 1992.

Clephane, Lewis P., *History of the Naval Overseas Transportation Service in World War I.* Washington, D.C.: Naval History Division, 1969.

Conrad, Joseph, *Lord Jim.* Boston: The Riverside Press, 1958.

De La Croix, Robert, translated from the French by James Cleugh, *Mysteries of the Pacific.* New York: The John Day Company, 1957.

Dick, H. W., and Kentwell, S. A., *Beancakers to Boxboats: Steamship Companies in Chinese Waters.* Canberra: Nautical Association of Australia, 1988.

Gibbs, James A., *Disaster Log of Ships*. New York: Bonanza Books, 1971)

____, *Peril at Sea*. West Chester, PA: Schiffer Publishing Ltd.,1986.

____, *Shipwrecks off Juan de Fuca*. Portland, OR: Binford & Morts, 1968.

____, *Shipwrecks of the Pacific Coast*. Portland, OR: Binford & Mort, 1957.

Gibson, Charles Dana, *Over Seas, U. S. Army Operations 1898 Through the Fall of the Philippines*. Camden, ME: Ensign Press, 2002.

Gibson, E. Kay, *Brutality on Trial: "Hellfire" Pedersen, "Fighting" Hansen and the Seamen's Act of 1915*. Gainesville, FL: University Press of Florida, 2006.

Grover, David H., *Captives of Shanghai: The Story of the President Harrison*. Napa, CA: Western Maritime Press, 1989.

____, *The San Francisco Shipping Conspiracies of World War II*. Napa, CA: Western Maritime Press, 1995.

____, *The Unforgiving Coast: Maritime Disasters of the Pacific Northwest*. Corvallis, OR: Oregon State University Press, 2002.

____, *U. S. Army Ships and Watercraft of World War II*. Annapolis: Naval Institute Press, 1987.

Gordon, Arthur, *The Years of Peril*. New York: Socony Vacuum Oil Co., 1994.

Hall, J. W., *The Law of Naval Warfare*. London: Chapman & Hall, Ltd., 1921.

Hoehling, Adolph A., *Lost at Sea*. Harrisburg, PA: Stackpole Books, 1999.

Holman, H. L., *A Handy Book for Shipowners & Masters*. London: Commercial Printing & Stationery Company, n. d..

Jackson, Walter, *The Doghole Schooners*. Mendocino, CA: Bear & Stebbins, 1977.

Landau, Henry, *The Enemy Within.* New York: Putnam, 1937.

Lloyds Register of Shipping. London: Lloyds Register of Shipping, various years.

MacLeod, M. K., preparer, Canadian Forces Headquarters Report, *The Prince Ships, 1940-1945.* Ottawa: Directorate of History and Heritage, 31 October 1965.

McNairn, Jack, and MacMullen, Jerry, *Ships of the Redwood Coast.* Stanford, CA: Stanford University Press, 1945.

Maugham, Somerset, "Rain." *The Complete Short Stories of W. Somerset Maugham, I, East and West.* Garden City, NY: Doubleday & Company, 1953.

Moore, Arthur R., *A Careless Word . . . A Needless Sinking.* Kings Point, NY: American Merchant Marine Museum, 1983.

Newell, Gordon, ed., *H. W. McCurdy Marine History of the Pacific Northwest.* Seatle: Superior Publishing Co., 1966.

Prange, Gordon W., with Goldstein, David, and Dillon, Katherine V., *December 7, 1941: The Day the Japanese Attacked Pearl Harbor.* New York: McGraw-Hill Book Co., 1988,

Reynolds, Quentin, *Officially Dead: The Story of Commander C. D. Smith.* New York: Random House, 1945.

Snapp, Jeremy, *Northwest Legacy: Sail, Steam & Motorships.* Lopez Island, WA: Pacific Northwest Heritage Press, 1999.

Sweetman, Jack, *American Naval History: An Illustrated Chronology.* Annapolis, Maryland: Naval Institute Press, 1984.

The Times Documentary History of the War, Volume III, *Naval- Part 1.* London: Printing House Square, 1917.

Webber, Bert, *Silent Siege III.* Medford, OR: Webb Research Group, 1992.

Weintraub, Stanley, *Long Day's Journey Into War.* New York: Truman Talley Books, Dutton, 1991.

Worden, William L., *Cargoes: Matson's First Century in the Pacific.* Honolulu, HI: University Press of Hawaii, 1981.

Wright, E. S., ed., *Lewis & Dryden's Marine History of the Pacific Northwest.* Portland, OR: Lewis & Dryden Printing Co., 1896.

Villiers, Sir Alan, *Posted Missing: The Story of Ships Lost Without Trace in Recent Years.* New York: Charles Scribner & Sons, 1974.

Articles

Coast Seamen's Journal, November 1927.

Collins, Edward, "Rendezvous with Destiny: The S. S. *Lurline*'s Pearl Harbor Voyage," *Amp&rsand,* Winter, 1991.

Grover, David H., "*Haida* Revisited," *Sea Chest,* June, 2005.

Inkersley, Arthur, and Brommage, W. H., "Experiences of a 'Blackbirder' among the Gilbert Islanders," *Overland Monthly,* June 1984.

Jahn, George W., "Survival by Lifeboat," *Amp&rsand.* Winter, 1991.

Jenkins, Francis G., "The Saginaw Steel Steamship Company and Its Steamers," *American Neptune,* v. 42, 1982.

March, Edward C., "Skinner and Eddy and Their 1105s," *Steamboat Bill,* Winter, 1994.

McCreery, David, and Munro, Doug, "The Cargo of the *Montserrat:* Gilbertese Labor in Guatemalan Coffee, 1890-1908," *The Americas,* January 1993.

Matthiesen, Hans O., and McMurty, Douglas, "Abandon Ship! The S. S. *Lahaina*'s Ordeal at Sea," *Amp&ersand,* Winter, 1991.

Monthly Weather Review, February 1927.

Oliver, Edward F., "Overdue - Presumed Lost," Naval Institute *Proceedings,* March 1961.

Pratte, Alf, "Cynthia Olson Five-part Series," *Honolulu Star-Bulletin*, 3-4, 6-8 December 1966.

Stadum, Lloyd M., "The *Haida* Mystery," *Sea Chest*, March 1958.

Newspaper Accounts

Daily Journal of Commerce

Japan Times

London Times

New York *Maritime Register*

New York Times

North China Daily News

Richmond (CA) *Record-Herald*

San Diego Union

San Francisco Chronicle

San Francisco Examiner

San Francisco [Maritime] *Guide*

Seattle Post-Intelligencer

Seattle Times

Archival Material

National Archives RG 45, Office of Naval Records and Library

National Archives RG 59, Department of State

National Archives RG 116, U. S. Courts

National Archives RG 118, U. S. Attorneys and Marshals

Miscellaneous Sources

Movement cards for vessels, National Maritime Museum, San Francisco

Pilot Chart for the North Pacific

Deck Log of USS *Conestoga*

Various Army-Navy files on *Cynthia Olson*

Correspondence, Dr. John Bow, in re name *Hai Da*

Internet Sources

Website: www.abovetopsecret.com/forum, as of 10-01-2010.

Website: The American Presidency Project, www.presidency. ucsb.edu.edu/ws/index, as of 3-01-2010.

Website: www.cargolaw.com, as of 10-01-05.

Website: Congressional Record, Extension of remarks, Hon. Walter B. Jones in House of Representatives, October 21, 1991, as of 9-15-2005.

Website: www.hsreemsnyder.com/derbyshire, as of l0-01-2010.

Website: Micronesia, www.janeresture.com/marakei/index.htm., as of 3-01-2010.

Website: Red Duster, Red Duster, www.red-duster.co/uk/Prince, 9, as of 1-01-2010.

Website: Red Duster, 9.

Website: Red Duster, 9.

Website: Spanish-American War Centennial, www.spanawar. com/Yucatan, as of 1-01-2010.

INDEX